Contributing Writers

Christine Borra, Kim Cernek, Mary DeVincenzi, Kim Harper,
Pam Jennett, Carole Larson, Jennifer MacLowry,
Connie Nagle, Heather Phillips

Editor
Denise Skomer

Illustrator
Ann Iosa

Cover Illustrator
Raquel Herrera

Designer
Marek/Janci Design

Cover Designer
Moonhee Pak

Art Director
Tom Cochrane

Project Director
Carolea Williams

Table of Contents

Go!

Introduction

Back to School provides beginning and experienced teachers with practical advice and classroom-tested ideas that are guaranteed to spark student excitement and interest at the start of a new school year. The advice and ideas in this book help you organize your classroom to make everyday tasks less time-consuming, freeing up more of your time to engage your class in fun yet effective lessons. *Back to School* is arranged in three sections:

On Your Mark: Organizational ideas and activities that can be implemented at any time.

Get Set: Ideas and advice for the days leading up to the first day of school.

Go!: Information for the first day and first weeks of school, including how to host and what to include in an effective and informative Back-to-School Night.

This book is a compilation of many teachers' ideas and activities. You may occasionally find that some activities do not apply to your teaching situation, philosophy, or style. Go with the advice that seems to be a comfortable fit for you. You may even find certain ideas will inspire you to create a totally new strategy that will work more effectively in your particular classroom.

School facilities also differ, especially from region to region. Check with your principal or custodian to approve the use of materials this book suggests, especially when an activity or idea involves putting something in or on a wall, window, or ceiling.

Look for this symbol throughout the book to find shortcuts designed by expert teachers.

This symbol signals tried-and-true information for getting parents involved, keeping them active in the education of their child, and/or maintaining a successful relationship with them.

Dog-ear the pages you want to come back to. Use sticky notes to remember where that fun icebreaker is. Paper-clip the lists of topics to include in your Back-to-School Night. Photocopy the tips on keeping your students on-task, and post them by your desk. Finally, keep this book close at hand. You'll come back to it again and again.

On Your Mark

*There is no such thing in anyone's
life as an unimportant day.*
—Alexander Woollcott

Manage Materials

What will I do with all this stuff? This question is more important than you realize, and the way you answer it may impact how smoothly your classroom runs. Managing the materials in your room can seem to be an overwhelming task. Piles of papers, pounds of pens and pencils, and a plethora of other goodies threaten to bury you and disrupt your daily schedule. But never fear! You can prevent the "Material Monster" from attacking. With a little planning, you will be in control and have your classroom running smoothly.

Store Bulletin Board Borders

Bulletin board borders are easily ruined, unless they are stored in a box specifically made for borders. Using frosting containers or baby-formula cans to store your borders is an inexpensive, compact alternative. Roll your borders, place them inside the container, snap on the lid, and then tape a short piece of the border to the front of the container to identify which border is inside. These containers stack easily, and the borders will not get wrinkled or torn.

Try to purchase a new border every few months. Select borders with different themes and colors. You will have a variety of choices to frame student work and create bulletin board displays. This is also an easy and quick way to add a new look to your classroom.

Store Bulletin Board Materials

An attractive bulletin board display adds excitement to any classroom, but keeping track of all your decorative supplies can be difficult. To ensure you will be able to reuse those great displays, store key pieces safely in inexpensive paper portfolios available at most art supply stores. Photograph your old bulletin boards before replacing them. Then, carefully take down the border, letters, and art while removing all old tape and staples. Place the parts of the bulletin board in a portfolio. Staple the photo of the bulletin board to the outside of the portfolio, and label the picture with the title of the board and the date you used it. Store these portfolios by stacking them in a large drawer or on a shelf or standing them side by side in a closet.

Create Theme Bins

Organizing materials for student use during the year requires forethought and planning. Create theme bins to accompany your instruction by decorating plastic crates or cardboard boxes. Label one bin *Reference*, and use it to store nonfiction informational books about the topic students are studying. Use a second bin to hold fiction books that coordinate with the unit, and label it *Related Reading*. Label a third bin *Project File*, and use it to store extra practice worksheets, independent-project ideas, and games or activities that coordinate with the unit. Allow students to browse these bins at their leisure. Place a sign-out sheet with each box so you can keep track of materials that need to be returned.

Organize Student Supplies

Help students learn to organize and keep track of their supplies with these ideas:

For Individual Students

- Obtain a small plastic storage box or shoe box for each student. Place an adhesive label on the outside of each box with the student's name on it (or if you use student numbers, write the number so labels can be reused each year). Next, have students fill their box with their supplies (e.g., pencils, crayons, scissors, erasers). Keep the boxes on a shelf alphabetized by student name. Encourage students to go to their box and get supplies as needed. Reuse the boxes each year, replacing the labels as needed.

- Collect large, wide aluminum cans (e.g., 1-quart vegetable cans). Cut off the lids, and sand the inside so that there are no sharp edges. Hot-glue felt or fabric to the bottom of the cans to keep them quiet against desktops and tabletops. Leave the labels in place, and invite students to glue scraps of wallpaper or fabric to the labels. Have students fill the decorated cans with their supplies.

For a Group

- Place small, inexpensive flowerpots at each student table or desk cluster. Fill the pots with markers, pencils, pens, and other supplies students may need during the school day.

- Hang three-tiered baskets (commonly used to hold vegetables) from the ceiling over each student grouping. Use extra chain or rope to ensure students can reach the baskets. Fill the baskets with supplies for students to share.

- Provide each table grouping with a plastic lazy Susan or a rotating cake base. Attach paper cups to the top with rubber cement. Fill each cup with school tools, such as glue, scissors, crayons, markers, pens, and pencils. Place a tool caddy in the center of each table.

 Ask your parent-teacher organization to donate inexpensive school supplies for your classroom. Place these community supplies in areas where students work in groups (e.g., learning centers and activity tables).

Organize Your Desk

You may not spend much time at your desk, but you will need to visit it to get at the key items it contains. If you can choose your desk, pick one that has several drawers. Set up at least one drawer for hanging files. Consider keeping the following supplies and decorative accents at your desk:

On Top of Desk
calendar
family photo
hole punch
paper-clip holder
paper clips (large and small)
pencils
pencil holder
scissors (at least 3 pairs)
small plant
stacking baskets or trays
stapler
tape dispenser

Inside Desk
large, black chart markers
fine-line felt-tip markers
drawer organizers
large and small envelopes
hanging file folders
ink pens
permanent markers
rubber bands
ruler
sticky notes
several kinds of notepads
staple remover
thank-you notes

Keep the items you will use most in your top drawer. Arrange the rest of the items in the drawers in order of necessity. If your desk has a drawer for hanging files, use the files for important school-related materials or for student portfolios. Label folders so you can find them quickly.

Place an in-basket on your desk for mail and notes from parents or the office. Put items in the basket as you receive them, and then go through the basket at the end of each day. The less you have on the top of your desk the better. A family photo and a small plant are enough decorative accents. Too many items makes your desk appear cluttered and unorganized.

 Place a lamp on your desk. Make sure the cord is in a place where students will not trip over it or knock the lamp off your desk. This simple touch will add a hint of home to your classroom, while providing you with additional light for reading and working.

Organize Overhead Projector Materials

Here are a few simple tricks to help you organize overhead projector markers, manipulatives, and transparencies:

- Glue magnets to the side of a small cardboard box—empty crayon boxes work well. Fill the box with overhead markers, and attach the box to the side of the overhead projector or the cart on which it sits.

- Tie a small apron decorated with fabric paints, buttons, and glitter glue around the top of the projector cart or the base of the projector. Fill the pockets with markers and the clear math manipulatives you use often.

- When presenting a lesson with several overhead transparencies, place a small sticky note on the edge of each transparency. Number the sticky notes in the order they will be used, and write an identifying code word or phrase to help you recognize each page. You will be able to easily identify which transparency comes next in your lesson without losing valuable time shuffling through pages to find the one you need.

Keep Track of Chalk and Dry-Erase Markers

Many classroom chalkboards and large dry-erase boards are magnetized. Obtain inexpensive storage containers equipped with magnetic strips, or make your own by gluing magnets to small boxes. Use these containers to store your chalk right on the board. Store dry-erase markers with the tip down to keep them from drying out. Find a lightweight cup (even a decorated sturdy paper cup will do), hot-glue a magnetic strip to the side, and use that to store your markers. If you use a lot of markers, pin the cup to the bulletin board or wall next to your board.

 Do not cover or place objects in front of the vents on an overhead projector. Some projectors will shut off automatically when they get too hot.

Establish a Community Use Policy

Many materials are shared among all the students in the classroom. Establish a "Community Use Policy" for sharing classroom materials. Include rules that have students treat materials with care, take turns with items, and return supplies to their proper places after use. Display this policy in a prominent place in the room, and review the procedures frequently. On occasion, students need to borrow classroom supplies for use at home. Record such use to ensure all materials are returned. Hang a laminated, rule-lined poster on a bulletin board near the classroom door, and attach a washable marker to the board with a string. If students borrow items to take home, have them sign their name on the board and write the item they are bor-

rowing. Upon entering the classroom the next day, they return the items and wipe their name off the board.

TAKE HOME		Rules:
NAME	ITEM	① Treat materials with care.
Joe S.	Markers	
Kevin L.	Scissors	② Share!
Tammy R.	Colored pens	③ Put things back where they belong.

 Trash to Treasure

Gathering materials for your classroom can be expensive and time-consuming. Many items you and your students will need for projects and activities can be donated by willing parents. Photocopy the Trash to Treasure letter (page 92), and simply highlight or circle the items on the list you would like donated. Send the letter home with students before or during the first week of school. You will be surprised at how much "treasure" you will accumulate to fill your cupboards.

 Use a clear hanging shoe organizer to hold classroom supplies, such as glue, scissors, markers, and crayons. The supplies will be easy to locate, and the prominent storage location makes returning borrowed items to the proper place a breeze.

Be Safe!

Use a backpack as an "Emergency Bag," and store it by the door you exit in an emergency. Include the following items:

- first aid kit—disposable gloves, cotton, antiseptic wipes, various sizes of adhesive and elastic bandages stored in a resealable plastic bag

- class list

- nametag necklaces. In advance, make a necklace for each student out of yarn or string and an index card. On the index card, include the student's name, allergies, phone number, emergency information, and parent release information

- dry-erase board and marker

- pencil, crayons, and paper

In an emergency, grab the bag and have the class exit immediately. At your designated area, take roll by distributing the necklaces. Any leftover necklaces will tell you who is missing. Put the leftover necklaces around your neck so you remember who the missing (or absent) students are. If you must wait before returning to your classroom, keep students occupied by playing games with your class on the dry-erase board. Or, in the event of an actual emergency, write key information on the board to display to other adults without having to yell. The pencil, crayons, and paper are for emergency notes and for students to use while waiting. In the event of an actual emergency, check students off the class list when they are picked up by their parents.

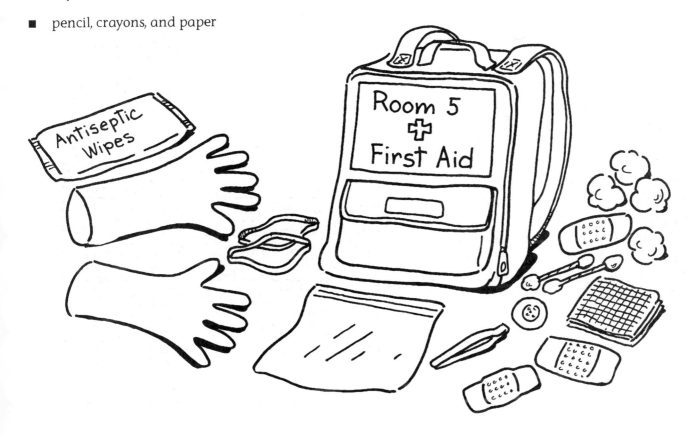

 Store your first-aid supplies in a fishing tackle box. Items stay organized and you can quickly inventory the box when the time comes for refilling.

11

Manage Time

Every teacher knows few things are more precious than time. How you manage it can mean the difference between an enjoyable, productive year and one that is hectic and frantic. Take a moment before school begins to develop a time-management plan that will save you valuable hours and minutes when every second counts.

Year-at-a-Glance

With so much material to cover and so little time, develop an instructional plan for the entire year. Begin by reviewing state standards and district guidelines, and, whenever possible, work with teammates at your grade level. Use this information to formulate an outline showing the material covered at your grade level. Focus on what you will need to teach in language arts, social studies, math, and science by duplicating a Year-at-a-Glance reproducible (page 93) for each curricular area. Create a teaching plan for each month by distributing the material to be covered into manageable chunks to be taught over the course of the year. This template will help you brainstorm activities related to each unit and develop different ways to coordinate classroom activities. Post this plan on a bulletin board or file cabinet near your desk. Keep yourself on track by referring to your plan at the beginning of each month.

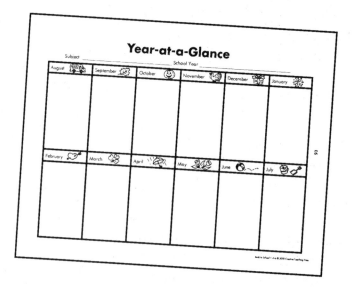

Identify Your "On" Time

Are you a morning person or a night owl? Believe it or not, determining your "on" time can make a difference in how productive you are. With so much activity taking place during the school day, you may find little time to take care of your routine business and organizational needs. Determine whether you function better early in the morning or late in the afternoon, and plan your day accordingly. Arriving at school a couple of hours before the students or leaving an hour or so after they head home will provide you with blocks of time to accomplish tasks that require your full attention.

Delegate Work to Parent Volunteers

Most parents want to be involved and are a great resource for making classroom life easier and better for all. Parents who work in the classroom will spread the word about all the hard work you do. By taking care of the more time-consuming daily-grind tasks (see the list below), they free up your time to run independent-learning centers, work individually with students, read journals, and do authentic assessment. Here are just a few of the jobs you can give parent volunteers:

She sent me a letter.

Timesaving Jobs
Organize room volunteers
Manage phone chain
Communicate special needs to parents
Organize committees

Workroom Help
Make die cuts
Cut paper
Bind books
Publish newsletter or class books (e.g., laminating, word processing, binding)

Classroom Help
Read with students
Check homework
Write and dictate stories
Work with individual students
Tear down and put up bulletin boards
Assist students with computers

Home Help
Assemble books
Trim laminated materials
Calculate book order
Word process
Make modeling dough

Tell parents that studies show parent participation to be a top indicator of student success.

13

Motivate Parents to Volunteer

Tell parents in your newsletters, in person, and at Back-to-School Night about

- influencing students positively. Many students perform better in school when they know their parents care and are watching.

- opening lines of communication. Volunteering helps parents have more informed conversations with their children and the teacher about what goes on in the classroom.

- creating their own feeling of success. They'll get the opportunity to be a contributing member of the classroom community.

- joining the group of supportive, interested parent volunteers. They have the opportunity to make friends with the other volunteers.

- gaining insight into their child's education. They'll learn how to work with their own children to help them do well in school and improve their children's skills.

Invite Parents to Work at Home

Many parents want to help, but cannot come into the classroom because they work or have other children at home. To help parents get involved, set up a parent work box. Write *Parent Take-Home Work* on several large manila envelopes, and laminate them. Number the envelopes to keep track of them and their contents. Place a clipboard inside the box with the envelopes and a numbered sign-out sheet. Invite parents to sign out an envelope on the clipboard. Be sure to include directions and a sample of what you want done. Include a due date to ensure you get the material back on time.

When you need volunteers for a special event, have students write letters requesting parents donate their time and talents. Personal notes from students often generate a better response from busy parents than a form letter.

Host a Volunteer Training Night

Set up a time to meet with your volunteers before they begin working in your classroom. Just as you set standards for students in your classroom, set standards for your parent volunteers. Explain your class discipline plan, and use the Volunteer Guidelines reproducible (page 94) or create your own to help parents understand your expectations. Ask parents to keep student information confidential. Demonstrate how to use equipment they may need, including office equipment. Take time to answer questions, and tell them they can talk to you about any problems that may come up in the future. Do tell them that their classroom visit is not the time to discuss their child, however. Be sure to tell parents your feelings about bringing other children into the classroom with them.

Show Your Appreciation

Above all, make sure your volunteers feel valued. Try these ideas:

- Put together thank-you treat bags on days when your volunteers will not expect it. Give one to each parent during a particular week. Try giving volunteers

  - a bag of Hershey's® Kisses™ and Hugs™ with a short note of thanks. Attach a note that says *You are a Lifesaver!* to a pack of Lifesavers™.

  - a class photo signed by each student.

- Always thank volunteers verbally when they are in your room. Be sure your students do the same.

- Have students write personal thank-you notes to parents who volunteer for field trips and room parties.

- Take a few moments to call parents who work at home. Let them know how much their time is appreciated.

 Tell parents that any time they can contribute is valuable, whether it's one hour a day, one hour a week, or one hour a month. This tells them that you respect their time.

15

Write Teaching Goals

Teaching is a craft. It requires practice, thought, and reflection. Begin your year by thinking about what you would like to accomplish. List several things you hope to achieve during the year. This may involve your teaching style, your classroom-management skills, your organizational plan, or your ability to work with colleagues. Prioritize this list, and focus on two or three items you feel are most important. Type these goals on your computer, and print several copies in large, fancy type. Tape one copy in your plan book, tape a second copy on the top of your desk, and place a third copy inside a closet or on a bulletin board near your desk. Each time you run across a copy of your goals, repeat them to yourself. Ask yourself what you have done that day to achieve each goal and make an effort to take a step closer to reaching your goals.

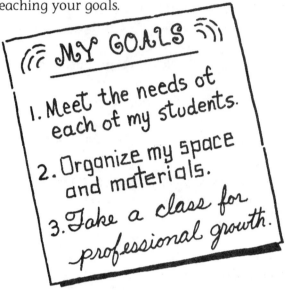

Frame Your Mission

Think about the kind of teacher you hope to be. List qualities and skills you need to achieve this goal. List your beliefs about teaching and learning. Using this information, write a personal mission statement expressing your vision and values. This mission statement will guide you in your decision making and direct your daily management of time. When you finish writing your statement, type it on the computer and print it on special stationery. Display your mission statement in a picture frame in a prominent place on your desk. Refer to it often as you organize yourself throughout the year. Weigh judgments and decisions against this belief system. It will prove to be a valuable road map to keep you on track as you move through each day.

 Find time to head to the teacher's lounge at least once each day. Try to share lunch or a cup of coffee with your colleagues and discuss the business of teaching. These informal meetings are good for your professional development and your mental health.

Manage Paper

The teacher's desk is a virtual magnet for paper. In a short period of time, you will find your work space covered with every size, shape, and color of the stuff. How do you manage the loads of paper you will encounter each day? How can you create a system that will clear your desk, yet still allow you to find the right form at the right time? The best way to keep your head above the paper flood is to build yourself a lifeboat before the first trickle begins to flow. Start the year with a plan to keep your paper organized.

Organize Important Information

Organize in a three-ring binder important information, such as class rules and procedures, permission slips, or information for new students. Use clear sheet protectors to store the original copy in, and use pocket folders behind the original to store photocopies. When you receive a new student or a parent requests a copy of a form, you will have the information easily available.

Make Lesson Plans Easy

Use a computer to make a lesson plan template, including elements of the schedule that do not change (e.g., lunchtime, recess, P. E.). Make two-sided copies, and use a three-hole punch to ready them for a binder. You'll only need to make minor changes from year to year.

 A great deal of mail accumulates in your school mailbox over the summer. Take the time to sort your mail before school begins. Make a file for catalogs, and refer to them later in the year. Prioritize any mail requiring some kind of action, and throw away all other mail that will take up space and clutter your desk!

Use Survival Lists

Use the Lists reproducible (page 95) to list and mark off tasks as you complete them. Use the *Survival List* on the reproducible, or give the blank list your own title. Lists might include *Materials I Need to Label, Papers I Need to Copy, Items to Give to the Office,* and *Questions I Need Answered.* At the end of each day, you will be able to look back over the day with a sense of accomplishment. Your time will be spent more wisely because a list will keep you focused.

Collect Student Work

Write each student's name on a three-ring divider tab, and put the dividers in a three-ring binder in alphabetical order. Place assessments, student writing samples, spelling tests, math samples, and other critical work in this notebook. At parent/teacher conferences, all you need to do is flip to that student's name and review the collected samples. When the next parent arrives, you are ready to flip to the next student and share his or her work. Also, when preparing report cards, it is easier to bring a notebook home than a stack of file folders.

Encourage Book Orders

Make photocopies of the Book Order Parent Letter (page 96), and keep the copies in a file folder. Every month, skim through the book-order form and list on the letter three good book choices with a brief description of why they would make a good addition to each student's home bookshelf. Fill in the appropriate dates and book-order information on the letter, make a copy for each student, have a volunteer staple each letter to a book-order form, and send the form and letter home with students. Parents will appreciate the time you save them and more of your students will order good books.

Use colored files, and assign each area of the curriculum a different color—red for math, blue for social studies, green for science, yellow for language arts. Use the corresponding colors in your plan book and grade book. Everything will be in plain view and you won't waste time searching for the right file.

Develop an Action Folder System

As "CEO" of your classroom, you have many demands on your time. Since you won't have a secretary or personal assistant, you'll need to find a way to manage all the paper that lands on your desk. Create an action folder system to help you stay organized. Purchase a three-tiered file box or a standing file organizer. Label manila file folders *Action Required, Hold,* and *File.* Every piece of paper that crosses your desk should fit into one of these three categories or be thrown away. Devote 15–30 minutes at the end of each day to review the three folders. Complete the work required to move the "Action Required" papers out of that folder. Make decisions about the placement of the

"Hold" papers, and file the papers from the "File" folder. Following this plan will keep your desk free of clutter and keep you on track for meeting school deadlines.

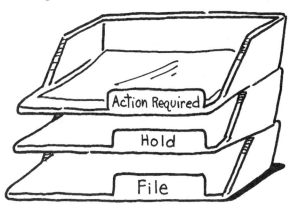

Create a File-Box Reference

You will often need to access personal information about students, such as phone numbers, addresses, and parent names. Rather than search through stacks of student files, prepare a handy desk reference for easy access. Purchase an inexpensive recipe box, some index cards, and alphabetical dividers. A small rolling phone file with alphabetized cards will also work. Create a card with the following information for each student:

- parent names

- home address

- e-mail address

- allergies

- parents' work phone numbers

- home phone number

- cellular phone and pager numbers

- emergency contact information

On the back of the card, list any information pertinent to contacting parents, such as parents' work hours and visitation schedules for divorced parents. Keep all student cards in your desk. Using a student reference box will make contacting parents hassle free.

Consider using a database on your computer to organize student contact information. Names, phone numbers, and addresses will be available with the click of a mouse.

Manage Centers

You have organized all the tools for learning in your room, created a workable time-management plan for yourself, and prepared for the onslaught of paper that will come across your desk. Now what will you do with the students? Before the students arrive for the first day of class, spend some time thinking about ways to organize them and plan how they will effectively use the classroom space. This section will give you some ideas on how to set up and manage centers and resources areas (e.g., computer centers and reading areas). For more ideas on managing students, see Establish Procedures and Routines (pages 55–63) and Foster On-Target Behavior (pages 64–70).

Schedule Groups at Centers

Assign students to groups, and give each group a color. (For more on grouping, see page 60.) Make a large and small circle from tagboard, and divide both circles into equal sections. Select a word or phrase to identify each center, and write the center name on a different section of the large wheel. Color each section of the small circle the same color as a group. Attach it to the center of the large circle with a brass fastener. Turn the wheel whenever groups are to move to a new center.

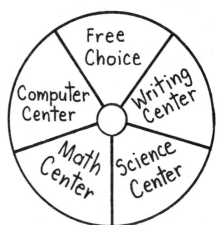

Create Center Signs

If you have specific center areas, center signs are a great way to designate the areas. Try these ways to display your signs:

- Attach center signs to long pieces of yarn, and hang one above each center. This keeps the signs off the work surface and out of the way. Be sure to hang the signs high enough for adults and students to walk under, but low enough for everyone to read them.

- Place your center signs in clear acrylic photo frames. On one side, display the name of the center, and on the other, display the directions for the center activity.

Organize the Classroom Library

The classroom library is a treasure trove for you and your students. The books you have so lovingly collected will be up for grabs and subject to the overstuffed desks, lockers, bags, and bedrooms of your students. How can you protect your books and ensure their safe return? Try these suggestions:

- Use a marker to write your name on the inside cover of all your books and initial several places within each book. This will remind students which books are yours and prevent your books from being returned to the wrong library. You may also wish to purchase an ink stamp with your name and stamp various places throughout each book.

- Create a card catalog for all your classroom books. Alphabetize the cards in a recipe box and label the box *Card Catalog*. Keep a

second recipe box next to the first and label it *Checked Out*. When students select a book to read, have them find the corresponding card, sign it, and write down the date. Then, have them place the card in the "Checked Out" box. Place a plastic bin or a cardboard box near the bookshelves. When students return their books, they place them in this container. Designate "Librarian" as one of your classroom jobs, and have students reshelve books and replace the cards in the card catalog.

Establish a Mail Center

Students may suffer from paper overload just like you. Help them manage papers and save yourself time and frustration in the process by creating a student mail center. Place inexpensive cardboard shoe organizers near the door of your classroom, and label each shoe space with a student's name. Place in the boxes forms, parent notes, graded homework, and any other items that need to go home. At the end of the day, have students pick up their "mail" as they get their coats and bags. Papers never reach their desks, and you are one step closer to helping correspondence reach home!

Finding books to fill your classroom library doesn't have to be an expensive task. Scout garage sales, rummage sales, and used book sales at libraries to stock your shelves. Once the year begins, ask parents to donate their children's unwanted books. Don't forget to take advantage of book-club bonus points, too!

Manage the Computer Center

Computers are excellent educational tools. They motivate students and can help them develop their problem-solving skills. However, they come with their own little bag of management problems, so here are some tricks to keep your computer-time routine on track:

- Use a kitchen timer to keep track of student time on the computer.

- Place a hanging file box next to the computer. Give each student a hanging folder labeled with his or her name. Keep student disks, worksheets, time logs, and other important computer papers in this folder. Students will be less likely to misplace this important information if it is always left near the computer station.

- Locate the computer near a bulletin board (away from a sink). Use the bulletin board to highlight assignments, note new software choices, and identify any key combination functions that students may have trouble remembering.

- Establish computer rules. Cover the proper care and use of the computer hardware and software. Print the rules and the consequences of breaking them on a contract, and distribute one to every student. Discuss the rules and consequences with students, and have them take the contract home to read and discuss with their parents. Ask both students and parents to sign the contract. Keep the contracts in students' computer folders.

- Train a group of students to be computer experts. When a student on the computer needs help, one of your experts can help solve the problem.

- When having students use the Internet, preview all sites they will be visiting. Spend time checking all the content on each Web site to ensure it is accurate and appropriate for students at your grade level. Never allow students to browse the Internet at will. Always bookmark sites that you will be using for teaching purposes, and only allow students to access bookmarked sites. Be sure to keep a watchful eye on the screen as students are using this tool. Most districts now have some type of Internet policy in place. Be sure to familiarize yourself with that policy and give a copy of it to your students and their parents.

- If your students will be doing a lot of word processing and publishing, give each student his or her own disk. This will protect students' precious work from being accidentally deleted from the computer hard drive or from other unforeseen accidents. Follow these simple steps:

  1. Buy preformatted disks for your computer type.

  2. Place each disk one at a time into the disk drive.

  3. Label the disk with the student's name as prompted by your computer.

  4. Remove the disk, and place on it a disk label with the student's name.

  5. Keep the disks in a disk box next to the computer.

  When students need to work on the computer, have them save their work to their own disk. At the end of the school year, pass the disks on to next year's teacher or erase, rename, and relabel them for next year's students.

- Keep a computer log near the computer. As students finish working, have them record the disk they used or the assignments they completed. This log will remind students where they were during their last computer session. It also reflects student progress and can be used as an assessment tool.

- Ask for computer-savvy parent volunteers to work with students on a weekly basis. These volunteers can provide one-on-one assistance for students and free you up to work with other students.

- Once a week present a new computer skill to students. Such skills include saving a document, printing a document, and opening a file. Demonstrate the skill, give students time to practice the skill, and then have them write about what they learned. Ask students to keep these technical journals in their computer folder so they can refer to them when working independently.

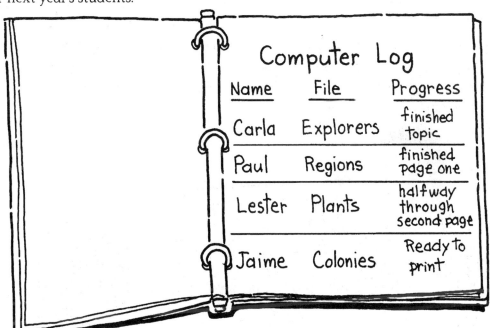

Computer Log

Name	File	Progress
Carla	Explorers	finished topic
Paul	Regions	finished page one
Lester	Plants	halfway through second page
Jaime	Colonies	Ready to print

If you use magnets in your classroom, be sure to keep them away from your computer center. Magnets can be damaging to computer equipment and destroy disks.

23

Create a Classroom Lounge

Create a comfortable space in the classroom to serve as a student lounge. Furnish the area with an old couch, comfortable chairs, beanbag chairs, or large pillows. Invite parents to donate old furniture or pillows for this area. Allow students to use this space for quiet reading, for informal discussion groups, or as a free-time space. Establish rules such as the following for using the space:

■ Use a quiet voice.

■ Maintain self-control.

■ Be considerate of all students in the lounge space.

■ Treat the lounge furniture with care.

Use lamps for lighting in the lounge. Current brain research suggests that flickering fluorescent lights may disturb students with attention deficit disorder. Incandescent lights, like those found in lamps, can have a calming effect on these students. Providing soothing light in the lounge will give all students using this space an energy boost and recharge their capacity for learning. Before creating such a space in your room, discuss it with your administrator to ensure he or she will support it.

Designate a Communication Corner

Designate one corner of your room as a communication corner. Use this area to resolve conflicts between students. Maintain a supply of tools such as the following for students to use when resolving conflicts responsibly and peacefully:

■ blank paper for journaling

■ pencils and pens

■ laminated copy of the Reminder Chart (page 97) for students to use as they work through a problem

Train students in the proper way to use this space. Encourage students to reflect on the conflict, accept ownership for their role, and develop a peaceful, constructive solution to the problem. Provide guidance for students as they use the corner during the first few weeks of school.

 Training students to solve their own problems will benefit both you and them. Students who are given positive strategies for handling conflict will function better in social situations, and you will not be consumed with sorting out everyone's issues.

Create a Learning Environment

During the school year, the students in your class may spend more waking hours in your room than they do at home. Spend some time considering ways you can create a positive learning environment in your room. Simple, inexpensive changes can make students feel comfortable, secure, and more open to learning. Be sure to check with your administrator or custodian before implementing any of the following ideas. Compliance with state and local safety codes should always be your first priority.

Don't Be Afraid to Personalize

Tour the houses or apartments on any given block, and you will find no two decorated exactly the same way. Why shouldn't classrooms reflect the same individuality? Here are a few inexpensive touches you can add to personalize your room:

- Fill your classroom with living plants. Green plants add warmth to your room and improve the quality of the air you breathe. Avoid adding flowering plants as they are more likely to affect students with allergies.

- Use self-adhesive wallpaper borders to brighten up drab walls.

- Purchase inexpensive framed art, or frame pictures you cut out of magazines. Posters and prints of animals, nature scenes, and inspirational sayings can be found at most craft stores. Simple plastic frames give these bargains a great finished look. Hang this artwork on the walls of your classroom and your students will feel right at home.

Your classroom is a reflection of you and your students. Take the time to periodically assess the state of your room and make changes to reflect how you and your class are growing and changing.

25

Use Fabric

Classrooms are filled with hard lines and rough edges. Paper covers most walls and bulletin boards. Try an original approach to decorating your room by adding fabric. These suggestions give you a variety of ways to bring a soft touch to your classroom:

■ Visit your local fabric store or the fabric department at a retail store. Purchase several yards of inexpensive, "fun" fabric. School prints are often available at the end of the summer. Cut the fabric for use as tablecloths on worktables.

■ Put curtains on the windows in your classroom. Inexpensive valances can brighten the room while adding a homey touch.

■ If the door to your classroom has a window, add a curtain for flair.

■ As an alternative to butcher paper, staple fabric to the bulletin boards for a backdrop.

■ Staple fabric around tables. Use the space under the tables for storage.

Throw a Room Setup Party

What better way to get acquainted with parents and students than to host a Room Setup Party? As soon as you have access to your class list, send each family a completed copy of the Invitation reproducible (page 98). Ask parents and students to join you in putting up bulletin boards, decorating the room, arranging desks, and organizing games and books. Provide your work crew with snacks and lemonade. Enjoy getting acquainted while you get loads of work accomplished.

Fabric adds wonderful, soft touches to the classroom, but it can be expensive. Rummage through the remnant bins at fabric stores, look for special discounts on discontinued prints, and find end-of-the-bolt markdowns. Your buying power will be greatly increased when you hunt for these bargains.

Create Usable Space Everywhere

Classroom space is always at a premium. Your mission is to find usable space in every corner, cupboard, and cubbyhole. Here are a few ideas that may help you stretch your square footage a bit further:

- Display work on the sides of filing cabinets. Magnets hold most papers in place, and you can turn an otherwise unattractive space into a showplace for student work.

- Hang student work and decorations from the classroom ceiling. A bent paper clip fits nicely into the grooved tracks of most drop ceilings.

- For especially high ceilings, string fishing lines diagonally from one corner of the room to the other. Use clothespins to clip work and decorations to the lines.

- An extra bulletin board can become an instant learning center. Place an extra desk in front of the board to hold reproducibles, manipulatives, or other materials necessary for the activity. Tack the instructions for the center to the board, and set students to work.

- Section off little niches in your room by placing file cabinets and cupboards at an angle. A well-placed cabinet can turn an unused corner into a quiet workspace or reading area.

- If you are feeling especially ambitious, consider having a loft built in your classroom. A well-constructed loft can create an upper reading area, while turning the lower area into a learning center or storage space. Be sure to check with your administrator or custodian before tackling such a project. Lofts will most likely require approval and inspection to cover safety and liability issues.

 Invite your students to give you suggestions on classroom arrangement. Students can be extremely creative and are often not blocked by traditional rules. They will offer you a fresh, unique perspective, and you may be surprised by the exciting creations they devise.

Create a Learning Environment

Arrange Student Desks

Student desks or tables make up the largest portion of furniture in your room. The way you arrange this furniture will affect the flow of traffic in your room and the way your students interact with you and each other. Review the desk arrangement options on page 29, and look through the following considerations as you plan the layout of your classroom:

Desk Arrangement

- Desks can be arranged in many ways. Create a floor plan of your classroom. Cut miniature desks out of paper, and experiment with arrangements in the floor plan. Try different arrangements, and make notes about things you like and dislike about each plan.

- Consider your teaching style and the types of activities you most often use with your students. Find a seating arrangement that best meets those needs.

- Keep your plan functional. You will need to have an unobstructed view of all your students, and students must be able to see all areas where you will be presenting information. Leave access for students to safely exit the room, and always allow space for you to move around each student's desk.

- Take into consideration your class size and the possibility that you may have new students added to your roster during the year. The cluster seating arrangement can accommodate 25–30 students by adding additional desks to each group. The U-shape arrangement can be adapted to a larger class size by adding one or two clusters in the center of the room.

Student Seating Strategies

- Get to know the needs of each individual student, and use this information when creating a seating chart. Seat your neediest students near your stronger students. Place those who are easily distracted closer to the front of the room. Have students who tend to fidget sit on the perimeter of the room.

- Be aware of those students who may be hearing or vision impaired and adjust their seats accordingly.

- Consider your students' heat and light preferences when arranging your seating chart. Some students prefer bright light or dim light. Some students are especially sensitive to cold or heat. These preferences may impact placement of students near windows or whether you seat them near heating or cooling units.

- If possible, try to give students the opportunity to sit in the front, middle, and back of the classroom at some time during the school year. You may be surprised how well a particular student will handle the challenge of sitting at the back of the room.

 Allow students to choose their own seats on the first day of school. This strategy will provide you with a wealth of information on social groupings, student behavior, and self-control.

Desk Placement

Clusters

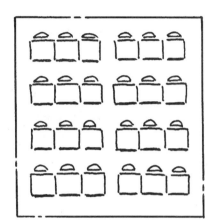

Table Groupings

Broken Circles

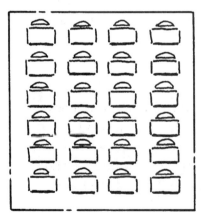

Traditional

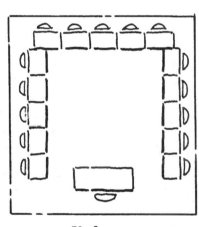

U-shape

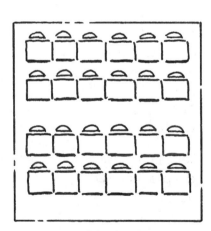

Double Aisles

Choose Pets for Your Classroom (or Not)

There are pros and cons to having pets in the classroom. Think about what you hope to accomplish with pets, and weigh the costs and benefits carefully. Classroom pets require a great deal of care—even a fish tank requires cleaning. Consider these points before you go shopping:

Pros

■ Pets give students an opportunity to be responsible for and care for another living thing.

■ They make a room cozy and homelike.

■ They can be incorporated into class activities, such as writing workshop or science, to make these activities more meaningful.

Cons

■ Many students have allergies to animals—even small ones.

■ Money for their care and feeding may come out of your pocket.

■ Furry friends require continuous care and cleaning.

■ Care for the animals on weekends and vacations requires management, and the pet is probably yours to take home over a very long break such as summer vacation.

■ A fish tank can stay and be maintained in the classroom, even over a very long break, but can be expensive to set up. Also, fish are like plants in that you either have the knack for keeping them alive or you do not.

Label, Label, Label

Label everything from drawers to boxes to containers. Labeling helps you find things quickly and easily. It also helps parent volunteers and substitutes. Keep these labeling ideas in mind:

- Labels do not have to be fancy. Use regular white labels or masking tape. Use a permanent marker so the ink does not rub off.

- Do not label everything in your classroom before school starts. Plan time on the first day of school for students to help you with this. They will be more responsible when putting things away. Laminate the labels before displaying them.

- For those items that you label yourself, glue photos, drawings, or pictures from school supply catalogs on sentence strips and label each illustration. Walk students through the classroom so they know exactly where to place each item.

Know Your Butcher Paper

Some teachers cover the entire wall in butcher paper because they like to, and some because water stains or age necessitates it. Before you cover large areas with butcher paper, locate all electrical outlets and light switches to avoid covering them. It does not matter whether you hang butcher paper in horizontal or vertical stripes, but do not cut the paper to the exact size. Cut the paper a little too long and fold the ends under, lining up the sides. This will give you a straight edge without a lot of measuring.

Create a Learning Environment

Communicate with Parents and Students

Communication is critical for running an efficient, productive classroom. You must effectively communicate information and expectations to your students. They will also need to feel they can openly share their thoughts and feelings with you. Establishing a good working relationship with parents is another key component of a successful school year. The beginning of the year is a perfect opportunity to reach out to both parents and students and build the foundation for a strong classroom community. Experiment with a variety of approaches to meet the needs of all your families. The following ideas, activities, and advice will help make your year go more smoothly.

Create a Classroom Contact List

Improve communication in your classroom by providing families with each student's address, phone number, and parents' names. A phone list will help you or your parent volunteers contact students' families when you need help on a class project or want to brag about a student's positive attitude. Lifelong friendships are built in the primary grades by parents getting to know each other and their students. Be sure to get permission from parents for each child you place on the list.

 Send home your classroom contact list with an inexpensive magnet for each family. Ask parents to use the magnet to attach the list to their refrigerator. This will reduce the number of lost lists.

Write a Welcome Letter

The students in your class and their parents will be anxious to get to know you. They will be wondering what you are like, what you enjoy doing, and what kinds of things you have planned for the year. Give them a sneak preview of yourself by writing a welcome letter before the school year begins. Write a letter to all students and their families telling them a little about who you are and your hopes for the upcoming school year. For an added touch, include a self-addressed, stamped envelope with your letter. Request that students write to you before school as well. Provide them with a Something about Me reproducible (page 99) to get them started, and encourage them to share something about themselves with you. You will likely be as curious about them as they are about you. Learning a bit about each other will build everyone's excitement for the new year.

Send Home Communication Folders

Have students designate a folder as their home/school communication folder. Each Friday, attach a copy of the Signature Log (page 100) to this folder and send it home with student work, notes, school information, and any other communication for parents. Ask parents and students to review the contents of the folder together. Ask parents to sign and date the log, and encourage them to write comments or questions in the comments section. Collect the folders each Monday, and check for signatures. Respond to any parent questions and concerns by making a phone call or following up with a note.

Recent studies on stress management show that focusing on positive thoughts can be beneficial to your health, and they will brighten your students' day, too!

Communicate with Parents and Students

Distribute a Newsletter

Maintain ongoing, upbeat communication with parents through your class newsletter. Send one home at least once a month—once a week, if you can swing it. Start with basic information, and add to it as you get in the habit of sending it home. Here are a few tips to keep in mind:

- Type your newsletter on your computer rather than handwrite it. It will look more professional and will be easier for your parents to read, no matter how perfect your penmanship. *Do not write in letter form—they will not read it.*

- To begin, open a word-processing document and save it as "Class Newsletter." Next, create a catchy title, like *5th Grade News*, *The Room 14 Chronicle*, or *Our Class Gazette*. Make your heading bold, and experiment with different fonts and font sizes. Each week, reopen the same document, change the date, add new items about curriculum, and recap last week's lessons.

- Separate your information into articles. Include titles and short summaries (e.g., *Reading, Writing, Pen Pals, Birthdays, Classroom News, School News, Social Studies, Science, Math*). Create a border around each main section to visually separate sections. This helps parents feel like they have time to read each article. Use a clear, easy-to-read font.

- Newsletters need to include the following: praise for the class (find something good to say), curriculum updates, dates to mark on family calendars, tips on how to help at home, and reminders of things students need to bring to school.

 If your school has a digital camera, use it to take photos of students at work in the classroom. Include these photos in your newsletter by inputting them directly into your computer.

- Print out your newsletter, and add a photo of a class activity. Parents will enjoy receiving pictures of what is taking place—even in black and white. Add photocopies of student work on the back. Invite students to nominate a few samples or work alphabetically from your class list, but rotate the work represented (e.g., by theme, by student, by content area). Reduce student work on your copy machine so four to six pieces can fit on a page. Include a brief sentence describing the assignment. Write the student's name by each piece.

- Include next week's spelling list in the newsletter. Encourage parents to work with their children to study words during the week.

- Include a *Parent Puzzler* section. Add a crossword puzzle, logic activity, or sample of what you are doing in class geared to an adult level. They will love it!

- Photocopy a class set of newsletters with only the titles of each section, and give one to each student. Invite each student to fill in the sections in his or her own words describing favorite events and activities from the past week.

- Send home newsletters on the same day each time. Parents will appreciate the routine. Be realistic about the time you have available to commit to publishing your newsletter. Begin with what is reasonable for your schedule and student population.

- Parent volunteers can help your students write and edit their articles. This is a great opportunity to involve parents who have basic computer skills.

- Invite parents to help you copy and collate the finished newsletters. Parents who are not comfortable working in the classroom will enjoy the opportunity to be involved in the production and distribution of an important piece of classroom business.

Communicate with Parents and Students

Use Agendas and Assignment Notebooks

Locate a central spot in your classroom to record the daily agenda, such as a chalkboard, a dry-erase board, or a laminated poster board. Write the daily schedule in this space each day. Include beginning and ending times for each activity, and keep to this schedule. This will keep both you and your students on task at all times. Be sure to list all events on the daily agenda, including lunch, recess, special classes, and assemblies.

The agenda should also include daily assignments from each of the curricular areas. Have students record these assignments in a notebook to help them stay organized and complete their work on time. Many districts provide a standard notebook for all students. If your district does not, develop a consistent system within your room. Here are a few suggestions for ways to handle assignment notebooks:

■ Create a template of your daily agenda for each day of the week. Make a class set of this agenda on a monthly basis. Ask students to

bring in a three-ring binder to hold the pages. Have students fill in the agenda each day and record any due dates.

■ Ask each student to purchase a small spiral notepad. Have students list each of the core curricular areas each day, note all assignments in each area, and write *no homework* in areas where no assignment is given.

■ Have each student purchase a stenography pad. Ask students to record short-term assignments in the left-hand column and long-term assignments in the right-hand column.

■ If your school supplies assignment notebooks, encourage students to use different-colored pens and pencils to record assignments for different subjects. Highlighters are also useful in denoting long-term assignment deadlines and crossing out completed work.

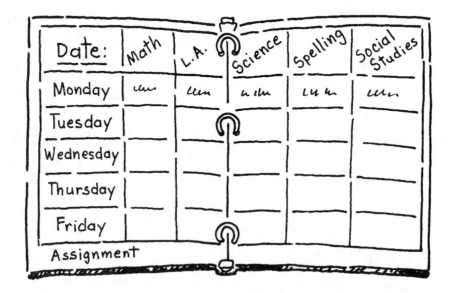

 When students have difficulty finishing assignments on time, ask their parents to review the assignment notebook each evening. Request that parents sign their child's notebook after he or she has completed all homework. This will ensure work is finished and communicate your concern about meeting deadlines to the parents.

Plan Ahead

Provide families with a monthly calendar to plan their schedules. Families are involved in so many activities—a calendar will help ensure that school events are included in the master plan. Write in school-wide events, classroom events, students' birthdays, celebrations, thematic topics, school spirit days, project due dates, field trips, and special materials needed on certain days. Photocopy this "master calendar," and send a copy home with each student. The calendar is a great communication tool.

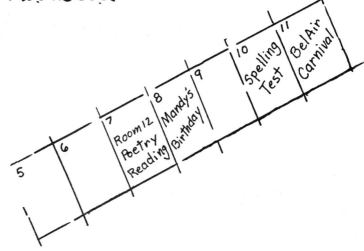

Write Informal Notes

Have you ever received a short note from a friend and suddenly found your whole day seemed a bit brighter? Why not share that same joy with parents and students? When returning graded papers to students, make a habit of occasionally adding a two- or three-line message about the work. Writing more than *Super, Great,* or *Needs Improvement* shows that you are really listening to what they have to say. Try to send an informal note to each student's parents about once a month. Write a few lines telling parents something wonderful

you observed their child doing, or tell them about something with which their child has struggled and is making improvements. Handwrite the notes on stationery to make them more personal.

> Dear Mr. and Mrs. Ryan,
> Mike had a great week!
> He received a 97% on his math quiz. I'm very pleased with his hard work!
> Have a great weekend,
> Mr. Monroe

Use a Parent Contact Sheet

Use the Contact reproducible (page 101) to document communication with your students' families. If you make a phone call, send a note home with a student, mail a letter, or have a spontaneous meeting with a student's parents, record notes about the conversation or contents of the note or letter on the sheet. This will save confusion later when you try to recall any agreements made on behalf of the student.

37

Schedule Routine Parent / Teacher Conferences

Many schools have fall parent/teacher conferences in which parents are given the opportunity to discuss the needs of their child(ren) with his or her teacher. These conferences are an opportunity to establish a good rapport with parents, review the child's strengths and weaknesses, and set goals for the future. Choose from these ways to have parents sign up for conferences or establish a schedule:

- Post a conference sign-up sheet at Back-to-School Night.

- Send home a note letting parents know conferences are coming up. Ask them to list three different days and times that they are available to meet with you.

- Assign everyone a time. Send home a note at least a month in advance, notifying parents of their time and inviting them to contact you if they need to change their time.

Manage Routine Parent / Teacher Conferences

Parents often feel uncomfortable with parent/teacher conferences. Make the conference comfortable for all. Make sure you have enough large chairs. Parents may feel awkward sitting in small student chairs. Offer the parents paper and pen so they may write down information. Begin the conference by telling them you are interested in their child. Ask questions about their child such as

- What are his or her hobbies at home? What does he or she enjoy most about school?

- What are your goals for him or her this school year?

- What do you see as his or her strengths and weaknesses regarding school?

Consider sending the questions home ahead of time for parents to return when they come to the conference. This gives parents time to reflect on their answers and gives them something to take to the meeting. Parents will feel like they are being listened to, and you will gain insight into each student and his or her family. Parents often arrive before their scheduled conference time. Provide a few chairs and a table in the hallway outside your classroom. Leave copies of current articles that would be helpful for parents to read. Also include copies of reading lists, suggestions for ways to read with their child, and other information you choose to share with parents. This is also a perfect opportunity to display class books, student projects, computer slide shows, and artwork.

Call a Parent/Teacher Conference to Settle Concerns

You may occasionally need to call an emergency parent/teacher conference. Establishing and maintaining open communication with parents is essential for meeting your students' needs. Parent/teacher conferences help you achieve this goal.

Do the following before the meeting:

■ Prepare notes about the student. Include observations of the student's strengths and areas of concern. Do not write anything about a student that you do not want a parent to read. Leave a section on the page to take notes during the conference. At the bottom of the page, indicate what actions you will take based on the information discussed in the conference (e.g., you will send home a weekly progress report about the student's work habits). Review these pages after the conference, and keep them on file for future reference.

■ Prepare a student work folder to share with parents during the conference. This will serve as documentation to support your observations of the student. If behavior is an issue, include documentation to show the frequency of the behavior. Student work, test data, and anecdotal information are also useful.

Parents are their child's best advocate. Develop a trusting relationship with parents. Listen to their observations and concerns. Their insights may provide critical data that will be useful in meeting students' needs.

A difficult conference may be emotional for both parents and teacher. Remain calm and professional in all situations. Initially, some parents may react defensively to concerns about their child's behavior or performance. Keep the best interests of the child as the constant focus of the meeting to disarm any negative feelings—yours or theirs. Occasionally, parents may need a day or two to reflect on the conference before they are willing to take steps you suggest. Make it clear to them that they have time to consider your suggestions. Continue to communicate a sincere interest in their child's well-being to reach an understanding that works for the parents, the child, and you.

Occasionally, a conference may involve other professionals (e.g., a social worker, a psychologist, a special-education teacher, an administrator). If additional staff members will be attending the conference, tell parents before the meeting. This will help prevent parents from feeling overwhelmed and outnumbered.

Communicate with Parents and Students

Prepare for Substitute Teachers

Sooner or later, even the most devoted teacher spends a day away from the classroom for training, a planning day, illness, or personal business. Proper planning in advance will save you time later. When students are on task and on schedule while you are gone, they stay that way when you return. The following ideas and advice will help you prepare efficiently and effectively for a day when you need to be out of the classroom and have someone else attempt to fill your shoes.

Find a Trusted Substitute

Find an experienced substitute teacher you and your students like. Schedule him or her for the days you know you will be out as far in advance as you can so your students typically get the same substitute. Your students will appreciate the continuity, and you will be able to entrust this teacher with your "real" lesson plans. With minimal disruption of their day, your students are more likely to carry on as they would with you than to view the day as "a day off."

Make a Substitute Fact Sheet

Create a one-page fact sheet for substitutes. Include important school information, such as the names of the principal, secretaries, and other teachers in your building. Highlight teachers of the same grade level or teachers who will be especially helpful should the substitute have questions or need assistance. Also include any special information that someone unfamiliar with your building may need. Such information may include

- how to order or buy a school lunch

- procedures for sending students to the school nurse

- how to contact the custodian

- how to use the intercom or phone system

- where the faculty bathroom is located

Keep a copy of this fact sheet in your substitute teacher folder (see page 41), or leave copies with your school secretary. He or she can give the substitute this helpful information upon entering the building for the day.

Substitute Facts
Lunch: Call in order by 9:30 a.m. ext. 421
Custodian: Mr. Ross ext. 431
Principal: Mrs. Jones ext. 451
Faculty bathrooms front hall office lounge

Create a Substitute Teacher Folder

Every teacher needs a substitute teacher folder. You never know when you may be out unexpectedly. The following items should be included in this folder:

- class list

- map of the school with key areas marked (e.g., yard duty, staff lounge, teachers' workroom)

- disaster information (e.g., fire drill/earthquake procedures)

- seating chart and name tags

- school forms (e.g., office passes, lunch tickets)

- directions to the staff bathroom

Your folder should also include a simple lesson plan for an unexpected absence. Your plan should include activities that are easy enough for any teacher to follow, such as a class set of a math sheet and directions for conducting silent reading, journal writing, or creative writing with a list of topics. Leave detailed instructions on how you have students read (e.g., silently, volunteers, in pairs). Include a list of students the teacher may call upon for help locating materials or learning other class procedures. Instead of having this substitute tackle important content areas for which you may have special projects in mind, photocopy an article of interest to students about a topic you do not intend to teach. A high student-interest level will help the substitute teacher maintain on-task behavior with your students, and students will perceive the teacher as one who brings them fun and interesting work. This will reflect well on you.

Use a two-pocket folder to organize all of the items for the substitute folder. Laminate the permanent pages for durability. Place student worksheets in one pocket. Place the laminated information sheets and lesson plan in the other pocket. Be sure to write at the top of your lesson plan *Use these plans if no other plans have been provided.* In the event you are absent, your classroom will carry on almost as usual.

 If you are ill or called away unexpectedly, consider e-mailing or faxing copies of your lesson plans to the school office.

41

Keep Need-to-Know Information Handy

Record procedural information on index cards. Laminate the cards for durability, hole-punch them, and place them on a key ring. Hole-punch the corner of your substitute teacher folder, and secure the cards to the folder. Breaking the information up this way will help your substitute teacher quickly find and make use of the resources you have left him or her. Information to put on index cards includes

- class schedule. Make a different card for each day of the week. Be sure to highlight any duties you may have, such as yard or cafeteria duty.

- classroom rules.

- rewards and discipline plan.

- list of helpful teachers and their room and classroom phone numbers.

- schedule listing students who leave the classroom for special services or teachers who come into the classroom to provide those services and the times for each.

- schedule listing assistants or other people who come to work in the room and the times for each.

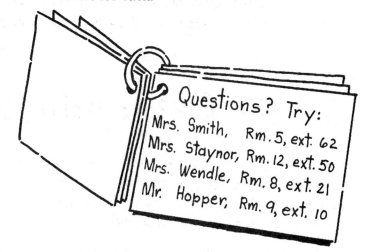

Make a Substitute Box

Write *Substitute Kit* and *Use anything in this box to help your day go smoothly* on a label. Place the label on a file box. Fill the box with a few good activities and related materials that are easy for someone unfamiliar with your class to do. Include a few good read-aloud books, a class set of fun paper activities (e.g., crossword puzzles, a book of riddles, math papers, a set of children's magazines or newspapers), and a simple art project (including all necessary art supplies). Add 8¹/₂" x 11" (21.5 cm x 28 cm) lined paper and 12" x 18" (30.5 cm x 46 cm) drawing paper to complete the box.

Include a list of students whom you trust for the substitute to ask procedural questions. This will utilize the strengths of your responsible students and provide the substitute with immediate assistance when small questions arise.

Go!

Happiness comes of the capacity to feel deeply, to enjoy simply, to think freely, to risk life, to be needed.
—Storm Jameson

You're Off!—The First Day

You have finally reached the moment of truth. All your hours of preparation and thought have led up to this day. You watch the busses roll in, feel the pounding of feet, and hear the laughter of children. What should you do next? Enjoy yourself! Incorporate these terrific ideas and activities into your plans and the first day will fly by with ease.

Go the Extra Mile for the First Day

The first day can be hectic. See the sample first-day schedule on page 44 for ideas on how you might schedule your day. Then, refer to the following tips to help it run smoothly:

- Make a separate lesson plan just for the first day. List the schedule on a board or a chart so you can mark off events as a class.

- Do not go over *all* of the rules the first day. Have students help write rules they think will help their classroom work better, and introduce the procedural dos and don'ts before the first time they will be needed.

- Leave a bulletin board blank for posting students' first work.

- Have a funny, lighthearted book ready to read.

- Let parents help organize the school supplies. Do not take up class time that could be better spent.

- Allow small amounts of time throughout the day for students to share summer happenings, instead of all at once. Students will enjoy the breaks.

- Take time to smile and let students know that you are excited about having them in your class. Share some of the fun activities planned for the year.

- Post a note with the dismissal time on the door for parents.

Dismissal Time 3:05 p.m.

Mrs. Allen Room 25

Sample First-Day Schedule

Time	Activity
8:30–8:45	Greet students at the door
	• Students sign in on classroom door
8:45–9:00	Take attendance
	• Use Creative Roll Call (page 45)
9:00–10:00	Class Meeting
	• Introduce Find Someone Who . . . (page 78)
	• Discuss expectations/Create class rules
10:00–10:45	Community building activity
	• Create a Class Motto (page 77)
10:45–11:30	Writing Workshop
	• Teach mini-lesson—overview of writing workshop
	• Write and conference quietly
	• Introduce sharing
11:30–12:00	Schultute—A German School Gift (page 47)
12:00–12:40	Lunch
12:40–1:10	Math
	• Teach problem-solving activity
	• Review grade-level skills students should know
1:10–1:40	Language Arts
	• School's Cool (page 80)
1:40–2:00	Lead a Classroom Scavenger Hunt (page 46)
2:00–2:30	P. E.
2:30–2:50	Teacher Read-Aloud
2:50–3:00	Pack up to go home
3:00	Dismissal

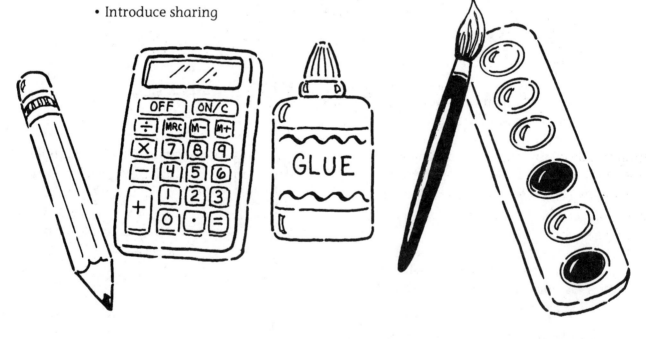

 Work with students on procedures before curriculum instruction. Research shows teachers who spend more time early in the year teaching classroom procedures and expectations make up the time later by losing far fewer minutes to problem behavior throughout the school year.

Meet and Greet Students

Don't forget that the first day of school can be a bit nerve-wracking for students. They may be familiar with many friends in their class, but undoubtedly some new faces will be in the crowd. Moreover, students will likely have been wondering about their new teacher for most of the summer. Help put their anxiety to rest by greeting each student with a handshake as he or she enters the classroom for the first time. Cover the door to your classroom with butcher paper. Write *Welcome* in large print at the top of the paper. Sign your name with a marker. As students shake your hand and greet you, hand them a marker and ask them to sign their name on the butcher paper. The new class list will be a great decoration and represent the first unifying activity your class completes this year.

Use Creative Roll Call

Getting to know your students is an ongoing process. Take advantage of every opportunity to learn more about who they are and what they like. One creative way to learn more about them is to use your daily attendance roll call. During the first few weeks of school, as you call roll, have each student share a "favorite" instead of saying *Here!* For example, students can tell you their favorite ice-cream flavor, color, animal, type of music, or sport when you call their name. Select a new category each day, and enjoy learning more about your students' likes and dislikes.

 To avoid mispronouncing student names on the first day of school, go around the room and invite each student to introduce him or herself. Have students pronounce their name and tell you what they prefer to be called. Remember to only allow appropriate, respectful nicknames in your classroom.

Lead a Classroom Scavenger Hunt

Students will most likely be unfamiliar with their new classroom. To avoid weeks of students asking you where to find supplies and reference material, have them participate in a classroom scavenger hunt. Pair each student with a partner. Give each pair a scavenger list of items found in the classroom. Adapt the Classroom Scavenger Hunt reproducible (page 102), making additions or deletions that fit your particular room design and arrangement. While students work to find all the items on the list, they will acquaint themselves with the layout of the classroom and learn where items can be found.

I Remember When . . .

Stories are powerful connectors for people. Think of an amusing story about yourself at the same age as your students. Relate this story or anecdote to students on the first day of school to acquaint them with you and demonstrate your ability to understand how they feel. Create a collage of yourself using pictures from your school days. Hang the collage on the front of your desk, and invite students to see you in your glory days.

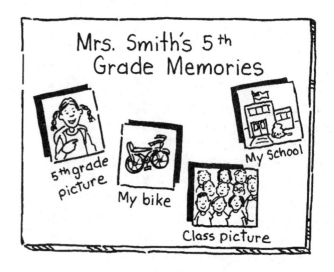

Mrs. Smith's 5th Grade Memories

5th grade picture

My bike

My School

Class picture

Consider leaving a map of the school grounds on each student's desk on the first day of school. Have students use a highlighter to mark the playground boundaries, where bus lines are, which doors to enter and exit the building, and the fire-drill route. Discuss this map with students, and have them attach it to the inside of their desk or locker for reference during the year.

Schultute—A German School Gift

School children living in Germany are given a large paper cone filled with candy and school supplies each year on the first day of school. The goody-filled cone is called a *Schultute* (pronounced *shool-'tootuh*). It symbolizes the wish that the student will have a rich education in the years ahead. Give each student a copy of the Schultute (page 103) and Cone Shape reproducibles (page 104) along with a piece of yarn and crayons or markers for decorating. Allot time in the morning of the first day of school for students to make and decorate their cone. Ask students to leave their empty cone on their desk when they leave for lunch. Fill the cones with inexpensive candy, a pencil, some erasers, and a welcome-to-school note while students are at lunch. They will be surprised and excited by the special gift.

 Manage School Supplies

If you have students bring in school supplies at the start of the year, use the School Supply Checklist reproducible (page 105) to keep track of students' school supplies as they come in. Have students use tape or a permanent marker to label their supplies and place the supplies in a designated area until you check them in. After two weeks, write a short generic reminder to parents and leave a blank space to fill in the specific supplies missing for each student. Photocopy the reminder, and use the checklist to quickly and efficiently make a personalized note.

From the first day, set the tone that the classroom belongs to all its members. Say *This is our classroom, not yours or mine.* Students will appreciate being an invested party, and everyone will be more willing to be involved when they feel ownership.

47

Bulletin Boards and Wall Displays

Bulletin boards and wall displays set the tone for the classroom. They celebrate work done, skills learned, and the people in the classroom. Be sure you clearly label everything you display so visitors can see at a glance the curriculum, skills, and volume of work represented. This section contains bulletin boards and other static or interactive displays specially designed for the first days of school, as well as how-tos for displaying student work all year long.

Two Approaches to Bulletin Boards

Use traditional or static bulletin boards to display student work and highlight current areas of study. This type of display typically provides an artistic backdrop for work. A colorful backdrop, a catchy title, some related artwork, and the student work create decorative appeal while validating the students' hard work.

Use interactive bulletin boards to give students a chance to work with information on display. A major advantage of such a bulletin board is its efficient use of space. The wall becomes a learning center, not just a showcase for work. Students also find these bulletin boards fun and exciting.

Try to change your bulletin boards regularly. They tend to fade and look worn after a couple of weeks. Your time and energy will be well spent re-creating your walls. Students will be excited by the new look, and parents and colleagues will enjoy reviewing your students' most recent accomplishments.

Make Word Walls

Learning to read "the writing on the wall" is an effective way to expose students to a wide variety of new and frequently used words. Word walls are an inventive and dynamic way to immerse students in language. Creating a word wall involves students adding a few words each week to a wall or bulletin board. Old words remain as new words are added. The result is a learning tool that is constantly being constructed and reconstructed throughout the year. Here are a few ideas for creating a word wall for your room:

Organize words
- alphabetically
- by word families
- by parts of speech (e.g., nouns, adjectives, adverbs, verbs)
- by commonly used words
- by commonly misspelled words or homophones
- by theme

Words for the word wall can be
- computer generated
- written on sentence strips or index cards
- written with a marker on butcher paper

To attach words to the wall, use
- pushpins
- double-sided tape
- tacky gum adhesive
- adhesive-backed Velcro

Arrange word walls
- in straight lines on the wall.
- inside a larger word or picture.
- against the backdrop of a large thematic drawing.
- on a moveable wall. (Cover a large piece of plywood with material or carpeting, and put adhesive-backed Velcro on the back of your cards.)

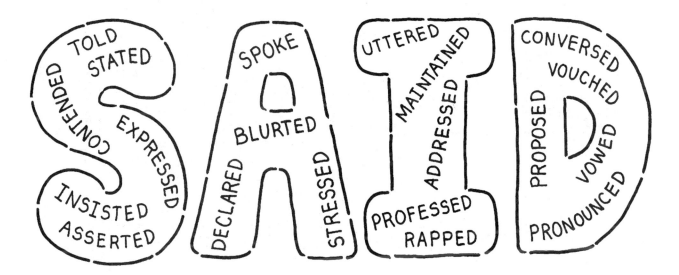

Values Board

Engage students in developing a positive learning environment by asking them to think through and reflect on important values. Write each of the following values on a large strip of poster board: *Respectfulness, Honesty, Courage, Civic Duty, Cooperation,* and *Perseverance.* Post these values on a bulletin board (as shown). Divide the class into six groups, and assign each group one value. Provide each group with two large index cards, a dictionary, a thesaurus, and any other reference materials you feel may be helpful. Ask the groups to research their value, and write a definition of the value in their own words on one of the index cards. Using the second index card, ask each group to write at least four examples of how that value can be demonstrated in the classroom. Use pushpins to connect string from each card to the corresponding value. Ask each group to present their value to the rest of the class. Have students discuss each value and the group answers from the cards.

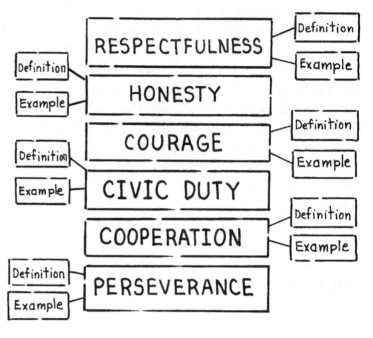

Times of Our Lives

Ask students to think about a memorable event in their life. Have each student write a newspaper article describing this time. Ask students to edit their article. Have each student copy his or her article on a Times of Our Lives reproducible (page 106). Students should include a photograph or drawing with their article in the space on the top left of the paper. Title a bulletin board *Times of Our Lives!* Display the student work.

Someone You Should Know

Organize students into groups of two or three. Assign each group the task of interviewing a staff member such as a custodian, principal, lunchroom supervisor, teacher, or school nurse. The class may brainstorm a common list of interview questions, or each group may develop their own. Preview each group's questions, and then send them out to set appointments for interviews. If possible, provide students with an instant camera to take a picture of their staff member. After students conduct their interviews, ask the groups to write a short profile paragraph about their person. Create a bulletin board in a hallway, the cafeteria, or in the front of the school building featuring the interview profiles and the pictures of the staff members. Invite other classrooms to learn more about the staff that makes their school special.

Goals for Success

Incorporate a sports-themed bulletin board into your back-to-school plan. Give each student a copy of the Goals for Success reproducible (page 107). Ask students to write one or more goals they have for the school year on the helmet. Invite students to decorate their helmet like their favorite team or come up with their own original design. Cover a bulletin board with green butcher paper. Create a goalpost out of yellow paper and a football shape out of brown paper. Show the football flying through the goalpost on one side of the bulletin board. Place the decorated helmets in the center, and complete your display by edging it with a sports-related border.

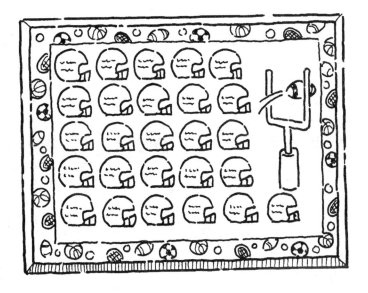

Reading around the Room

Attach wide adding machine tape in a single strip around the walls of the classroom using tape or tacky gum adhsive. Each time students read a book, ask them to record their name and their book's title and author on the tape. Challenge students to read enough books to fill the tape by the end of the school year.

Logic Board

Select a small bulletin board that can be devoted to the same topic all year. Call it the "Logic Board." Each week post a new logic puzzle for students to solve. Place a box under the board for students to put their answers in. Give them the whole week to work on the answer. Have students explain their answer and write their name on a piece of paper to be put in the answer box. Create a deadline of Friday at noon for answers. Check the answers, and record the names of the students with correct responses on a piece of paper. Post the names on the board as the "Brain Busters" for the week. Spend a few minutes on Friday afternoon discussing how the problem is solved.

Thematic Border

Invite students to help you create a custom-made bulletin board border. Have students use paint and sponges (or potatoes cut into thematic shapes), stamps, stickers, and crayons or markers to create designs on white or colored adding machine tape or narrow strips of butcher paper. Laminate the finished border for durability.

Thinking outside the Box

Introduce students to the phrase "thinking outside of the box." Tell students that this refers to challenging yourself to view items and situations in a new way. It may also refer to stretching one's limits. Ask students to consider things that may be outside of their normal comfort zone. Some examples include

- speaking in front of a group of people

- leading a group to accomplish a goal

- trying an unfamiliar art medium

Have students choose one goal that stretches them to think outside their "box." Have students write that goal on an index card and indicate a time frame for completing the task. Create a bulletin board with a large, 3-D box in the center. Attach each student's card to the center box with a piece of string. Encourage students to monitor their progress and indicate their success by drawing a smiling face in marker over their index card when they complete their chosen task.

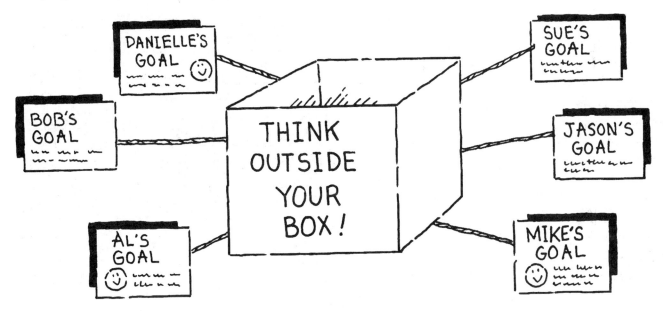

Who We Are

Ask students to think of an image or symbol that best represents who they are, or who they are striving to be, and develop a sketch of their symbol. Post a large piece of mural paper on a bulletin board. Invite students to use paints, markers, crayons, and colored pencils to transfer their image onto the mural paper. Have students sign their name next to their drawing.

53

Fall into a Good Book

Try this display idea on a wall near your reading corner:

1. Create a 3-D tree out of wire, brown butcher paper, and green butcher paper. Place it against a bulletin board. Staple fishing line around the tree and into the wall to make the tree stable. Alternatively, sponge-paint a tree on construction paper, or use a pre-made tree.

2. Cut out assorted colors of construction or butcher paper leaves, or wait until the first day of school and invite students to sponge-paint fall leaves to be added to the board.

3. Write titles of books the class reads on the leaves or display the book covers or books on the bulletin board along with the scattered leaves. If you make the board prior to the first day of school, attach the books you plan to read with T-pins (one on the top and bottom) and hang real fall leaves.

4. As you read the books or add books, invite students to write book reviews to add to the board.

5. If you plan on changing this board with each season, show the changing seasons on the tree.

6. Make a "growing" border out of the title of each read-aloud book using small construction paper rectangles to resemble books.

Solve the Problem of Hard Walls

Some classrooms have hard walls that resist staples and tacks (e.g., cinderblock walls). Here are several solutions that do not involve power equipment or staple guns:

■ Purchase a roll of cork at a home improvement store. Nail or hot-glue the cork to the wall.

■ Nail ¼" (6 mm) sheets of plywood to the wall, and cover with butcher paper or fabric.

■ Use tacky gum adhesive to hang laminated posters and artwork.

■ Use adhesive-backed Velcro for pocket charts and posters. Place one side of the Velcro on the wall and the other side on the item you will display.

■ Brush rubber cement on the back of butcher paper or laminated materials. When you take the piece down, the rubber cement will rub off easily.

Establish Procedures and Routines

When you think of the many tasks that need to be accomplished in the average school day, you wonder how in the world everything gets done. The answer is simple—give students clearly defined procedures and routines. Students thrive in a well-structured environment in which they understand the rules and expectations. They are able to become active participants in the running of the classroom, and as a result they become more invested in their own learning. Try some of these tried-and-true ideas for getting your classroom to run smoothly.

Teach Transitions

An effective transition signal that quiets students so they can hear the next set of directions you give does not involve raising your voice. A raised voice encourages more raised voices. Try these simple tips to get students' attention in a positive way:

- Choose a unique noisemaker, such as a tambourine, a cowbell, or a rain stick—the more unusual, the better. Use this sound to signal transition times between activities or as a notice for students to stop and listen for further directions.

- Use a windup music box to get your students' attention. Every Monday, wind up the music box. When you need the class to be quiet, open the music box. As soon as they have quieted down, close the box. Explain that if there is music left in the box by the end of the week, the class will earn a reward.

- Choose a special class word. Write one letter of the word at a time, and teach students to be seated by the time you write the last letter of the word. If your class has a team name, that works well. For example, if your class is named Sea Stars, write on the board S-e-a-S-t-a-r-s. All students should be at attention by the last s.

- Hold up your hand and count backwards from three to one. If students are not quiet when you reach one, begin timing them. Keep track of the number of seconds you must wait for students to quiet down. Write that time on the board, and keep a running total. Subtract the time from student recess or free time. Have students wait out their "transition time" quietly.

- Create a two-part code phrase that can alert students to be quiet and listen for further instruction. You say the beginning phrase and students complete it. For example, you say *I need peace and . . .* and students finish *quiet!* or you say *Surf's . . .* and students say *up!*

Plan for Student Absences

Inevitably, students will be absent on occasion. Plan ahead by creating a system for collecting and organizing assignments. Here are a few ways to ensure that absent students stay in touch:

- Keep copies of the We Missed You reproducible (page 108) in a central location in your room. Assign two or three students a week to the job of collecting homework for absent students. Have them fill in the assignments and collect handouts for each day a student is out.

- Pair each student with a homework buddy. The buddy is responsible for collecting handouts and recording the assignments and lessons the absent student missed during the day.

We Missed You

Name _____ Date _____

While you were out, you missed some important work. Please make up the work and turn it in by the date written on the bottom of this sheet. If you have questions or need help, please see me.

Subject	Assignment	✔ When Completed

Due date _____

108

Create an Assignment Account

No matter how dedicated your students are on the first day, inevitably someone will miss an assignment during the course of the year. Keep a record of missing assignments so you can help students eliminate problems and stop bad habits. Document missing work in a binder. Make a page for each student. Use the Assignment Account reproducible (page 109) for this purpose. When a student doesn't turn in an assignment, have him or her record the date and describe the missing work. Keep next to the binder a box filled with copies of the Missing Assignment Form (page 110). After students record their missing homework in the binder, have them take home a parent form. The next day, students return the signed form with a completed copy of the missing assignment. Staple the form to the student assignment, and place both in the binder. This binder holds students accountable for their completed work and is useful to share with parents at conference time to show any patterns of incomplete assignments.

Get Students on Track

Students in the intermediate grades often have difficulty organizing their materials and completing assignments in a timely manner. By giving them and their parents some strategies for getting and staying focused, you can establish positive, lasting habits early in the year. Send home the Get Your Child on Track reproducible (page 111) with each student. Write the following information on a chart, and display it in your classroom:

Getting on Track at School

1. Copy all assignments in your assignment notebook.

2. Review each item and take out all materials necessary to complete each one.

3. Carefully pack your backpack with all materials necessary to complete your homework.

4. Pack your assignment notebook in your backpack.

> Getting on Track at School
> - Copy all assignments in your notebook.
> - Review each item and take out all materials to complete each one.
> - Carefully pack your backpack with all materials necessary to complete your homework.

Create Schedule Reminders

Keeping track of all the special pullout classes, such as band, speech, reading assistance, and others, can be difficult for everyone. Help students remember when and where they need to be by providing them with their own schedule reminder. Write each student's schedule on an index card. Use a different-colored pen for each day of the week. Laminate the cards, and tape them to the top of students' desks. As students familiarize themselves with their weekly schedule, provide gentle reminders by glancing at the cards as you move around the room.

Don't worry about winning students over. Students love a teacher who provides them with a safe environment in which to learn. Communicate your expectations and back them up consistently.

Create Classroom Jobs

Classrooms operate much like families. Each individual has certain rights and responsibilities within the classroom unit. The responsibilities involve working together to perform the daily tasks necessary to help the unit function efficiently and effectively. Classroom jobs are a means of naming, delegating, and managing these tasks. When students complete classroom jobs, they develop a sense of active participation in the classroom family. You are also relieved of the added duty of managing daily chores. Many chores need to be done each day. Some jobs will only need to be completed once or twice a week. The first step in determining what jobs you will need is to brainstorm a list of all the tasks performed regularly. Such a list might include the following:

- taking attendance

- passing out and grading papers

- straightening the classroom library

- returning library books

- watering classroom plants

- feeding class pets

- carrying playground equipment to recess

- filing completed and corrected work

- stuffing student mailboxes

- writing homework on the agenda or assignment board

- running miscellaneous errands

Write your job list on an overhead transparency. Ask students to review the list and add any additional suggestions. Once your job list is complete, copy it onto a large poster and laminate it. Hang the chart in a prominent place in the classroom. Write students' names on the poster with a washable marker.

 As students participate in the running of your classroom, they become independent learners. Each time you do something *for* your students, consider whether they could do the task themselves instead. If the answer is yes, add the task to your classroom job list.

Assign and Rotate Classroom Jobs

Students will be anxious to jump in and get to work. Now comes the task of establishing a routine for assigning and rotating the jobs. Make sure the method you select is manageable for the entire year. Here are a few suggestions for job assignments:

- Place two large jars on your desk. Label one *Job Jar #1* and the other *Job Jar #2*. Write each student's name on a small card. Place all the cards in Jar #1. Draw cards from the jar to fill each job. Place the drawn cards into Jar #2. Each week, select a new group of students to fill the jobs. When the first jar is empty, reverse the process by drawing names from Jar #2. This way, students will be assigned jobs an equal number of times.

- Place slips of paper with all student names in a hat. Select a name, and give the student ten seconds to select a job. Repeat this process until all jobs are filled. Do not replace the names of students who have been selected. Draw new names each week until all students have held a job. Begin again by filling the hat with all students' names.

- Create a giant construction paper or butcher paper ladder, and attach it to the wall. Label each rung of the ladder with a classroom job. Write each student's name on a footprint cutout. Place the cutouts in a large envelope at the bottom of the ladder, and place another large envelope at the top of the ladder. Begin by choosing cutouts for each job. Tape the footprints on the rung for the corresponding job. Each week, move students up the ladder one rung and select a new footprint from the envelope at the bottom of the ladder to fill the first job. Place the footprint from the top rung into the envelope at the top of the ladder. When the bottom envelope is empty, exchange it with the envelope at the top.

- Find an old, worn pair of blue jeans. Use your own, or pick up a pair at a second-hand store—the more tattered the better. Decorate a bulletin board with a multicolored background, and title the display *The Work Crew*. Staple the old jeans to the middle of the board. Label index cards with each of your classroom jobs. Staple these cards to the legs of the jeans. Write each student's name on a sticky note, and rotate students through the jobs alphabetically. Each week, move the sticky notes as students move to a new job.

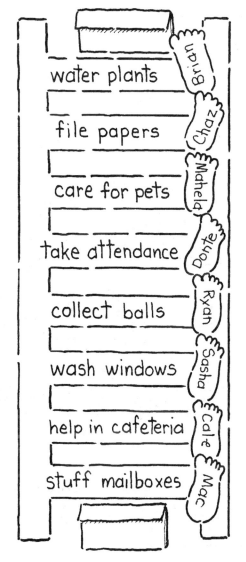

Establish Procedures and Routines

Create Student Groups

Cooperative grouping is an effective way for students to learn how to work together to achieve a common goal. Collaboration or "group work" provides a vehicle for students to problem-solve, improve oral communication, and learn how to be a successful group member. Classroom groupings also promote positive peer relationships, creating a nurturing environment for learning, while diminishing common classroom problems.

Students can and should be in more than one group at a time. Here are a few different grouping options:

- A family group consists of four to five students who remain together for the entire school year. They meet daily to write in their journals, fill out assignment notebooks, collect homework for students in their group who are absent, and problem-solve classroom issues. This group provides a constant base for students and helps form positive, lasting peer relationships.

- An academic group is a temporary group established to meet short-term goals. It may consist of several students who need to master a particular skill. This group comes together to work on a specific skill and then disbands.

- Groups may also cross grade levels. Having students from the primary grades work in groups with students from the upper grades allows both younger and older students the opportunity for growth. These types of groups are well suited for reading projects.

- An interest group is formed when students share a common like or interest and come together to do further study. This group is especially useful for curriculum-based project groups. For example, students studying "community" for social studies may group themselves according to interest. Several students may wish to learn more about community government. Some may wish to learn about fire and police. A third group may select to study families. Each group focuses on their interest area, and then they share their research with the whole class.

- A service group is a small number of students selected to work together to complete a specific task. The task may be within the classroom, on the school campus, or in the community. A group may come together to organize the classroom library or to clean the school playground or community park. This is a temporary group that is usually assigned one task.

Students may be grouped by ability in either homogeneous or heterogeneous groups. Remember that a variety of grouping options provides students with the best overall learning experience. Always provide ways for students to assess their group's progress. Rubrics such as the Rate Your Group reproducible (page 112) and journal entries are two ways to effectively assess group progress.

Plan Field Trips

Field trips are special days. They require careful planning, as early as possible. A well-planned field trip will encourage more parents to volunteer for the next one and you'll have fun, too. Try these tried-and-true ideas for field-trip success:

- Have students dress alike for a field trip. At least have students all wear the same color pants and shirts (e.g., blue jeans and white shirts). For a terrific beginning-of-the-year class-unity project, have each student bring in a white T-shirt. Dye all the shirts bright yellow—the dye is inexpensive and directions are on the box—and have students use sponge paint to decorate their shirt with themes that reflect your expected field trips (e.g., animals for the trip to the zoo, a baseball bat for the trip to the game). Encourage students to bring in a shirt that is a little big for them so they do not grow out of it by the end of the year. Wash the shirts yourself after each trip or have a parent volunteer do it. If you send them home, these beloved shirts may not come back.

- Find out what field trips other teachers in your grade level are taking and what trips teachers in the grade levels before you have taken. Avoid taking students places they went last year, and coordinate with teachers in your own grade level to travel together. Sharing buses and the responsibility for phone calls or fund-raising can be a big help. If you are a new teacher, find out what field trips the previous teacher took (and what units they were tied to) and decide whether you want to continue these traditions.

- Divide the class into small groups with a parent chaperone assigned to each group. Give each adult a list of the children he or she is responsible for, and give each driver a map with written directions. Do not assign yourself a group. Your job is to oversee the class and the adults.

- If you are taking a bus to your destination, bring a box with trash bags and baby wipes. Have it on board in case of motion sickness.

- Plan only a short time for lunch. Children eat quickly, and most field-trip destinations are not properly equipped for recess. Twenty minutes is probably enough.

- Always take a first aid kit on field trips. Use a fanny pack to hold the medical supplies. If you are on a field trip where your groups will be separated, create a kit for each chaperone.

 Do not schedule field trips for Mondays or Fridays. These are transition days. Weekends can be stressful for kids, even if it is "good" stress. On Mondays students need a day to get back into the school frame of mind, and on Fridays they are already anticipating the weekend.

Establish Procedures and Routines

Manage Bathroom Breaks and Getting Drinks

Requests to go to the bathroom or get drinks may interrupt lessons and learning. However, you need to know where your students are at all times, and you need to know if students are abusing this privilege. These teacher-tested systems encourage students to get drinks and use the bathroom as they need to and allow you to monitor students without disrupting learning:

■ Write each student's name on a craft stick. Divide the name sticks into two containers, one labeled *boys* and one labeled *girls*. Decorate three other containers. (Cans or plastic cups work well.) Label one container *Boy's Bathroom*, label the second *Girl's Bathroom*, and label the third *Drinks*. When students need to use the restroom or get a drink, they move their stick into the appropriate container. If someone's stick is already in the container, students should wait for that person to return to the room. This system allows you to know where students are at all times.

■ Write each student's name on a clothespin. Attach a piece of rope to the wall next to the door. Have the rope hang down so all students can reach it. Attach the clothespins to the rope. Create cardboard icons to represent the boy's bathroom, the girl's bathroom, and the drinking fountain. Hang these icons on or near the classroom door. When students need to use the restroom or get a drink, they take their clothespin from the rope and clip it to the appropriate icon. If students break the rules or have behavior problems using this privilege, clip their clothespin to your shirt or pants. The students will then have to ask for their clothespin before using the bathroom or getting a drink. You will be able to closely monitor their coming and going.

■ Make two large cardboard keys. Label one key *Boys* and one key *Girls*. You may also wish to color-code the keys blue and pink. Hang the keys on hooks near the classroom door. When a student needs to use the restroom, he or she takes the appropriate key. Upon returning to the classroom, the student replaces the key on the hook.

■ Research shows that drinking water helps students maximize brain power. Invite students to keep a filled water bottle on their desk so they can have a drink whenever they need one. Generate with your students a list of rules for water bottles (e.g., water only, they may only fill it during their recess, lunch, or free time).

Establish Student Journals

Regardless of the specific purpose, all journals serve as a place of reflection. Students reflect on what they learn and, in the process, gain a better understanding of how they learn. The following examples describe several types of journals and how you can use them in your classroom.

- A reflective journal is used to express personal feelings. Students may use it like a diary. Pose questions for students to answer, or allow them to write freely about what is going on in their lives.

- A literature journal is used to respond to literature questions, keep a running list of books students have read, write book reviews or book reports, and maintain a list of books students would like to read.

- A math journal is used to keep math homework, practice word and logic problems, solve equations, and take notes on new math skills.

- A home/school journal allows students to write entries and have their parents respond in written form. The entries may focus on current-event discussions or classroom news and activities or alert parents to curricular areas in which students need assistance or improvement.

- A technology journal is typically used to keep track of instructional notes on using the computer and any software students are using. Students record shortcuts for working with software and keep track of the programs they are currently working with in class.

Foster On-Target Behavior

Some of the most important lessons you will teach the students in your class are not found in a text-book. They involve the ability to develop self-control and manage conflict in their everyday lives. Teaching students strategies for functioning in a group, asserting their beliefs in an appropriate manner, and problem-solving solutions to conflicts gives them essential tools for becoming productive members of the classroom community. Assist students in developing appropriate behavior patterns by creating incentive programs in your classroom. When setting up an incentive system, include rewards for individual, small-group, and whole-class achievement.

Both the small-group and whole-class achievement rewards promote positive peer pressure and camaraderie. Post an easy-to-read description of the system, and inform those who visit and are involved with your students of your policies.

Discuss and Define Class Rules

Make classroom rules meaningful and memorable to your class by involving students in the process of generating the rules. During the first days of the school year, brainstorm with students their classroom rights and responsibilities. Based on these rights and responsibilities, discuss acceptable and unacceptable classroom behavior. Then, generate as a class a set of class rules, keeping the following in mind:

- Keep rules brief.

- Generate broad rules.

- Keep rules few in number.

- Use a positive tone (i.e., tell what to do, rather than what not to do).

Test the usefulness of the rules and establish clear definitions of them by suggesting hypothetical situations in which students demonstrate acceptable and unacceptable behavior, and discuss as a class the rule to which each situation applies. Reword the rules as necessary to make sure all situations are addressed. Finally, number

the rules and post them within all students' view. When students are in violation of a rule, simply hold up the number of fingers corresponding to the rule to avoid interrupting your lesson or train of thought. Because students were active in creating the rules, they will be much more likely to abide by them. The following is an example of an effective set of rules.

Rule 1: Be responsible.
Rule 2: Be respectful.
Rule 3: Be resourceful.
Rule 4: Be a risk-taker.

Use Alternate Solution Sheets

Unfortunately, you will not always be present to hear and know the events that lead up to every conflict between your students. The fact is you will know very little about how most conflicts arise. What you will hear are each person's perspectives on what has happened as a result of the conflict. Use the Alternate Solution Sheet (page 113) to diffuse some of the emotion surrounding conflicts and help students try to understand how a solution can be reached. Ask each person involved in the conflict to fill out the form. Meet with students to hear their perspective of the situation, and lead them toward a peaceful, fair resolution to the problem. If behavior problems are a common occurrence for particular students, have them take home their Alternate Solution Sheet and discuss it with their parents.

Pass the Talking Stick

To conduct effective group discussions, students must communicate in a productive and orderly manner. Use a "talking stick" to signal which student has the floor. Decorate an empty paper-towel tube with paint, streamers, construction paper, and sequins. As you conduct a group discussion, give the stick to students as permission to talk. Students must be holding the stick in order to speak, otherwise they should be listening. Students may request the stick when they want to contribute to the discussion, or the stick can be passed around the group in an orderly fashion. Using a talking stick will give all group members a fair chance to participate and share their thoughts.

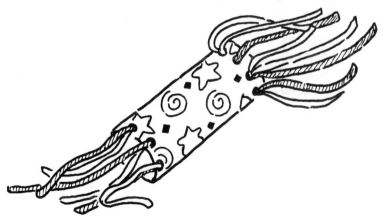

Work with the class for the first few weeks, reinforcing rules and procedures until routines are firmly established. Have students practice lining up and transitioning quietly. Be certain they know what to do with finished work and what to do when their work is done. The time spent at the beginning of the year pays off with time gained throughout the rest of the year.

Foster On-Target Behavior

Individual Incentives

Use the following ways to recognize individual students who exhibit exemplary behavior:

■ Brainstorm with students privileges or small prizes they would like to earn. Add the favorites to the blank Cool Coupons (page 114), and photocopy the reproducible on neon-colored card stock. Cut apart the coupons, and display them in a clear container. Keep a large supply of Cool Coupons available to reward students who are staying on task, helping a friend, or demonstrating appropriate behavior.

■ When you want to reward students for accomplishments such as bringing back permission slips or homework on time, helping a friend, or being a good listener, give them a ticket. Have students write their name on the ticket and place it in a jar. Each week, draw a few winning tickets. Award small prizes (e.g., pencils, erasers, special markers) to the winners. Empty the jar each week or accumulate tickets all year.

■ Encourage students to be organized and finish all their assignments on time. Keep track of students who turn in 100% of their homework each month. At the month's end, provide a breakfast complete with pancakes, juice, doughnuts, cereal, or sweet rolls for those students. If students are bussed and cannot arrive before school for breakfast, have pizza delivered for a lunch in the classroom. Recruit parents to help you with this undertaking. This incentive program can also be used for good behavior in the classroom, on the playground, or in the lunchroom.

■ For selected students who need additional positive reinforcement, photocopy on card stock the How Am I Doing? reproducible (page 115), and write the class schedule in the Task column. Sit down with each student, and show him or her the card. Explain that, at the end of each lesson or time slot, you will reward his or her appropriate behavior during each class period with a check, star, or sticker. Have the student tell you what that appropriate behavior will look like. Put the student in charge of taking responsibility for his or her own learning and not interfering with the learning of others. Challenge students to make progress each day. Tape a card to the corner of each student's desk. For the first week or so, check in with students after every activity. As they progress, you can check in a few times a day. Cross off class periods from the chart once students consistently receive stars and stickers for two weeks.

Small-Group Incentive Programs

Using small groups to encourage on-target student behavior is smart teaching. Peers encourage each other to meet and exceed your expectations, and working together towards points or other rewards can bring a group together. Here are a few ways to reward groups who are working well together:

- Draw a large box in the corner of your chalkboard or dry-erase board, and divide the box so that there is one section for each group in your class. Award points to the first few groups seated, attentive, and prepared for the next lesson following a transition. At the end of each week, give a reward to the three groups with the most points. For example, if you use raffle tickets, give each student in the group with the most points three tickets, each student in the group with the second-most points two tickets, and so on. If you award privileges, consider having a luncheon with the groups and bringing a dessert treat for each student.

- Have each group generate a name (suggest themes at the start of each new grading period or unit) and write it on a large piece of construction or butcher paper. Invite the groups to decorate their banner, and then display the banners above the groups or on the walls. As students work together, award stickers or stamps to deserving groups on their banner. Count the stickers or stamps at the end of each week, and invite the group that earned the most stickers or stamps (for that week) to take a trip to the prize box, or offer some other suitable reward.

- Photograph each group, and display the pictures on a bulletin board, each with a different color of 9" x 12" (23 cm x 30.5 cm) construction paper stapled beneath it. Add stickers or stamps to the corresponding paper as each group earns recognition. At the end of the week, award a small prize to the three groups with the most stamps or stickers. Change the paper at the end of each week.

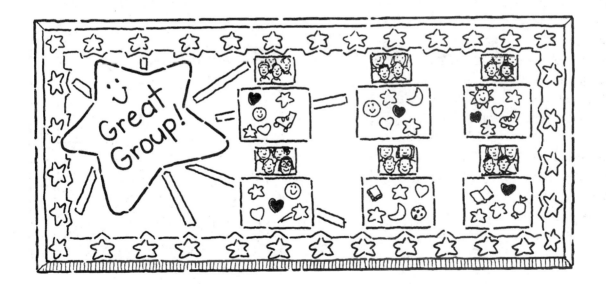

 Encourage independence by giving students options for activities when their work is finished (e.g., read a book, write a letter, work at a center). Keep their choices simple for the first few days of school, and then gradually increase their options until they have at least five or six different choices.

Whole-Class Incentive Programs

Rewarding a class for a job well done can help encourage individual students to do their best for the benefit of the class and brings the group together to work towards a common goal. Listed below are a few easy-to-implement systems for rewarding a class that is functioning well as a group. For each system, have the class agree in advance on the reward they are working towards (e.g., a pizza party, a movie in class).

- Draw a ladder by the chalkboard. Each time the class exceeds expectations, move a footprint cutout one rung up the ladder. Award a prize when you place the footprint on the top rung. Alternatively, use a real ladder (which has fewer steps) and have the class earn five tally marks before you move the footprint each step.

- Keep a jar in an easy-to-spot location of the classroom. Add a marble to the jar every time the class exceeds expectations. Award the class a prize when the jar is full.

- Make a paper chain with a link for each point students must earn towards their prize. Hang the chain high enough to keep it safe, but low enough that students can reach it with your help. Every time the class deserves recognition for their behavior, have a student break the next link in the chain. When the last link is broken, give students their reward.

- Create a scene on the bulletin board representing the award. At the bottom of the scene, add enough elements for each point the class must earn for the prize. Each time the class deserves recognition for their behavior, have a student move an element into the scene, until all the elements have been moved into the scene and the class earns the reward.

Get Them off to Work

There are many times during the course of the day when students have extra time. These "off-task" moments can easily lead to wasted time and disruptive behavior. Run interference for your students by giving them alternative activities to fill their free moments. Here are a few ideas for things to do:

■ Write a series of problems on the chalkboard before students enter the classroom each morning. Examples may include math word problems, grammatically incorrect sentences for students to correct, simple geography questions, numerical equations to solve, short writing prompts, or a combination of all of these. Have students maintain a notebook for the problems. The morning business of attendance, returning library books, and reading any communication from parents is easily addressed while students are actively engaged in their assignment.

■ Have students brainstorm a list of things they can do when they finish assignments early. Display this list prominently in the classroom. Some examples are solving math problems, writing articles for the class newsletter, reading independently, practicing multiplication facts, and practicing handwriting skills. Have a general list for the whole class, or give each student an individual list, depending on his or her own needs. Another alternative is to write a list on the board that changes as the curriculum changes.

September 18

Answer these questions:
1. What is the capital of Idaho?
2. Name the Great Lakes.

Correct this sentence:
i dont no where i left my homework

Hold a Weekly Class Meeting

Institute a weekly class meeting to review procedures, deal with classroom business, and discuss any problems troubling students. Allot 10 to 15 minutes each week for this meeting. Try having a different group of students run the meeting each week or month. Meet with the planning team the day before the meeting and develop an agenda. Choose one person to take the minutes of the meeting. Display the minutes prominently in the room where all can read them.

Foster On-Target Behavior

Teach Classroom Problem Solving

Help students solve their own conflicts by combining a little direct instruction with some smart environment choices. Here are a few of both:

■ Divide a common sequence of events into four or five steps, and list them on a chart or a large piece of butcher paper. Have the first step show a common classroom situation, such as *John, Rachel, and Susan agreed to work on a science project together.* Show the last step in the chart with a conflict like *"I'm never working with you again," said Susan as she stormed away angrily.* Ask students to consider what steps may have led up to the disagreement. Have them brainstorm the events to fill in the chart. After the chart is complete, discuss a better way the situation could have been handled.

■ Discuss empathy with students by asking them to verbalize their feelings. Encourage them to reflect on how their actions make others feel. Work to establish an understanding of cause and effect in relation to actions and the way those actions make others feel.

■ Encourage students to be accountable for their own actions. Have students practice using "I" statements instead of "He" or "She" statements when discussing disagreements. Ask students involved in a conflict to write what happened. Then, invite these students to come together and discuss what they wrote. Monitor the discussion, and mediate a solution to the problem. Students will learn to see how their own actions influence situations and the way others react to them.

■ Create a "cool-down zone" in the classroom. Equip it with paper and pencils. When students are involved in a conflict, have them go to the cool-down zone and write about their problem. Ask students to describe their problem and develop a solution they feel would resolve the issue. Give students five to ten minutes to work through their feelings. Meet with all individuals involved in the conflict, and mediate as they decide on an appropriate conclusion.

■ Promote a positive classroom climate by instituting a "No Put-Down" rule. Encourage students to respect others with their language as well as their actions.

Track Growth

Each year your students will learn new academic and social skills, and you will need to describe this growth to them, to their parents, and to your administrators. Here are some terrific ideas for capturing their growth on paper so you can refer to it later when someone catches you in the hall with a question.

Use Anecdotal Notes

Set up a binder to file notes on behavior throughout the year. Have a section for each student. File several copies of the Kid Watch reproducible (page 116) in each student's section. Throughout the day, record on sticky notes academic and behavioral observations of students during activities. Jot the name and the activity at the top of each note. At the end of the day, transfer the sticky notes to the appropriate columns of the Kid Watch reproducible to help track growth and needs. Look for patterns in behavior (e.g., always responsible, frequently off task, eager to answer questions). Privately discuss needs for growth with individual students at recess or after school, and then look for this growth. Share your notes during parent/teacher conferences to support your observations. If behavior is an issue over time, photocopy the student's page at the end of the day and send it home for parents to read, sign, and return to school the next day.

Kid Watch

Name _____   Week beginning _____

Language Arts

Math

Other

Comments

Parent Signature

Teacher Signature

Put your class list on a clipboard for each subject. The clipboard can be used to evaluate work on the spot, especially for cooperative group work. Grades can be transferred to the grade book at a later time.

Write Weekly Goals

Foster personal responsibility by having students write weekly goals for themselves. Ask students to write both academic and behavioral goals. Steer students toward breaking larger goals into smaller, manageable chunks that can be achieved each week. Have students also write one or two ways their goals can be achieved. Refer to the goals each day during the week. Write notes on the assignment board reminding students to work toward goals. On Fridays, guide students through an evaluation of their weekly goals. Have them write an evaluation statement under each goal. The following Monday, have students review the previous week's goals and write new goals for the week. Keep each student's goals and evaluation statements in a journal. Students will benefit from periodically flipping through their journal and assessing where they have been and where they are heading.

> Goal:
> I will try not to fight on the playground.
>
> Friday evaluation:
> I had trouble on Wednesday. I will try to not lose my temper.
>
> Goal:
> I will try not to fight on the playground.
>
> Friday evaluation:
> I did better this week. I played with different people! ☺

Teach Student Self-Assessment

Student self-assessment tools such as rubrics and journals are excellent ways of maintaining data on student growth. Try both of these tools:

- Class-generated rubrics are especially meaningful since the act of defining the learning goals is part of the process of defining the rubrics. Assign students a short activity in the content area for which you are generating a rubric. Then, use papers without names from previous years, or generate a high, medium, and low paper yourself. Do not use a paper from a current student. Invite students to discuss the differences in the papers and define the areas in which the papers excel or need work. Have students assign merit numbers to each definition. Guide the discussion to include the areas you will be assessing. For example, point out how clear handwriting makes the high paper easier to read. When the class has defined each level of the rubric (as many as five levels, as few as three levels), invite students to examine their own paper and use the rubric to assess their own work and that of two friends. Have them write why they felt they earned the rubric score they did and what they intend to do differently next time to improve their score (e.g., *I will use correct punctuation in my writing*).

- Journals give students time to reflect on various tasks. From time to time, write questions for students to elicit assessment information for specific standards. Periodically collect and read the journals, and then meet with students to discuss their entries.

Take Photographs of Student Work

A fun way to track student growth is to photograph their projects and products at various times throughout the school year. Date and label the photographs, and file them in student portfolios. You will see at a glance the growth and development of student skills. If you have access to a digital camera, create a computer-file portfolio for each student complete with digital photos of his or her work. Photographing student work is an excellent job for willing parent volunteers. Ask your volunteer shutterbugs to schedule times when they can come to your room and photograph students at work and student-made projects.

Create a File Box

Create a file box for 3" x 5" (7.5 cm x 12.5 cm) index cards with each student's name on a dividing tab. Place stacks of 3" x 5" cards and felt-tip pens in various locations around the room. Throughout the day, if a student shows improvement in a task or displays a work habit that needs improvement, jot down the student's name and a brief note. At the end of the day, date the cards and file them in the box. These provide a helpful resource during parent/teacher conferences or for reference during phone calls home.

Create individual grade or behavior reports for students on your computer, and place copies in student portfolios. Create class reports to show evaluations of class projects and group work.

Create Portfolios

Portfolios provide physical evidence of students' ability to meet content standards and learning expectations. Label a legal-size file folder with each student's name, and store the folders in a location accessible to you and your students. Have students select pieces of their work to include in their portfolio. Periodically meet with each student to review the work in his or her portfolio and assess growth.

Create a Teaching Portfolio

Portfolios are a wonderful way to track student growth, but they can also be a powerful source of professional development for teachers. Begin a portfolio for yourself at the beginning of the year. Here are a few suggestions of things to include in your portfolio:

- copies of units you write and teach

- copies of lesson plans

- pictures of bulletin boards

- copies of your evaluations with your principal

- goals you have written for yourself

- complimentary notes from parents or colleagues

- notes you made about things you learned in teaching various lessons

- a teaching journal that you keep during the year to record your activities, plans, goals, feelings, and reactions

When the school year is over, spend some time reviewing the materials in your portfolio. Consider the information when you write new teaching goals for yourself and plan instruction for the next year.

 Schedule time each day to write in your journal. Model for your students by writing in your journal while they write in their journals. Keep to this schedule until it becomes a habit. The entries will help you focus your thoughts, and they will be a valuable resource for your professional growth.

Build Community

Laughing and playing together is a vitally important part of learning together—even in the intermediate grades. Making time to do so in a purposeful way builds a sense of classroom community and pride. The following activities are geared towards creating a classroom that works and learns cooperatively.

Make Birthday Books

Celebrating birthdays makes each individual student feel special. Making birthday books is one way to involve all students in creating a special gift for the honored girl or boy. Give each student a half-sheet of white construction paper. Have students create a one-page card for the birthday student. Ask students to write one positive statement on the card or a compliment, a wish, or a friendly comment. Include your own page with a special birthday note. Collect the cards, and invite a parent volunteer to make front and back covers for the birthday book. Put the book together by hole-punching the top or sides of the book and tying it together with pieces of string. The birthday student will have a lasting wish for a happy day from the students in your class. Remember those students with summer birthdays and birthdays that occur during school breaks by celebrating before or after breaks and recognizing half-birthdays.

Write a Class Song

Have students brainstorm a list of the things that are unique or interesting about their class. Using this list as inspiration, have the class write lyrics for a class song set to the tune of a familiar piece of music. Another alternative is to divide the class into small groups. Give each group the task of creating their own original song to represent the class. Ask each group to perform their song for the whole class.

Write your students' birthdays and half-birthdays in your plan book. This will help you remember their special days. If you write personal notes to students or give special stickers, paper-clip these in your plan book.

Recognize a Student of the Week

Recognize a different student each week of the school year as the "Student of the Week." Ask students to bring pictures of themselves at various ages, awards they have won, examples of favorite items, or pieces of their collections, such as stamps, dolls, cars, or rocks. Have students think of descriptive statements about themselves that include physical traits, likes and dislikes, and hobbies and write these statements on sentence strips. Post the strips around the room, and display the student's special items in a central location. Treat the students' collections as if they were a museum exhibit. Classmates are encouraged to look and enjoy each other's items but not to touch any piece brought in for display. Provide a mailbox made from a simple shoe box, and place it on the featured student's desk. Ask each student to write a positive comment to the Student of the Week about his or her collection and place it in the mailbox during the week. Begin the year by featuring yourself. You will be surprised how much even older students enjoy show-and-tell.

Write a Class Mission Statement

One way to pull your class together as a team is to create a mission statement. Begin by telling your students that a mission statement includes the values and beliefs that are most important to the class as a whole. The statement tells who you are and what you hope to become. Ask students to list words and phrases that describe your class. Have them include descriptions of what they would like to become. Write all student responses on chart paper. Review all responses with students, and prioritize items, eliminating those deemed less important. When you have narrowed the focus to four or five key components, write the mission statement with the class. You may wish to phrase it like the Preamble to the Constitution (e.g., *We, the students in _____*) to incorporate elements from the social-studies curriculum. Copy the finished product on poster board, or use a computer to create a professional-looking document. Print a copy for all students and their parents. Hang a copy in the classroom, and have students read the mission statement every morning after reciting the Pledge of Allegiance.

Play a Beach-Ball Game

During the first week of school, get students working together and bonding with this fun activity that requires a beach ball and a stopwatch. Bring students to a large open area, such as a gym or playground, and give one student a beach ball. Instruct students to work as a unit to keep the ball in the air for as long a period of time as they can. The only other rule they will need to follow is that everyone in the group must touch the ball at least twice. Students may think this sounds easy, but they will soon determine that the task will take some planning and organization. Use the stopwatch to time students as they work with the ball.

Observe which students are the natural leaders and organizers of the group. Also, note any potential personality conflicts that may arise within the group. Keep a record of the group's longest time keeping the ball in the air. This is a great activity to pull out periodically during the school year. Use it whenever students need a break, such as during standardized testing.

Teach Cooperative Juggling

Have your students develop gross-motor coordination and teamwork while working on their juggling skills. Organize students into groups of four or five. Give each group one small beanbag. Have each group stand in a circle, arm's length from each other. Have students toss the bag around the circle as quickly as possible without dropping it. When students have perfected passing one bag, add a second to the mix. Continue adding beanbags until the group can juggle four at once.

Create a Class Motto

Encourage the class to list things that successful students do. This list might include listening to others, cooperating, thinking critically, thinking creatively, setting goals, communicating clearly, working independently, working cooperatively, solving problems, motivating self and others, and appreciating diversity. Invite the class to decide which ideas they want to

include in their class motto, and select two ideas from the list to complete the sentence *If I can ____ and ____, I can do anything!* Ask small groups of students to illustrate the class motto, and display this work on a bulletin board in the classroom. Encourage the class to say their motto daily.

Get into Gear— The First Few Weeks

The first few weeks of school are filled with developing procedures and establishing rules. Don't forget to take some time to get to know your students and help your class come together as a group. The following activities offer suggestions for you to get acquainted with your students while jumping into the business of academics.

Find Someone Who . . .

Give each student a Find Someone Who . . . reproducible (page 117). Explain to students that they will be moving around the room trying to find someone in their class to fit each category on their list. They may ask you or classmates about a particular category on their chart. For example, students will need to find someone who plays a musical instrument. Tell students they must ask a specific question and not *Do you match anything on my chart?* When students match a category on the chart, they should sign their name in the appropriate square. Students may use the same person only twice. After everyone has filled out as much of the chart as they can, spend some time discussing the answers to learn a bit more about each student in the classroom.

Name _____ Date _____
Find Someone Who . . .
Directions: Get a signature in each box. Each person may sign no more than twice.

plays a musical instrument	has a pet	plays a sport	belongs to a club or group	has lived in another state
has lived in another country	has a special collection	has been in a contest	has grown something in a garden	has an unusual hobby
has two or more brothers	has two or more sisters	likes to keep their room clean	wants to become a professional athlete	has been stung by a bee
loves math	took a summer school class	read at least two books over the summer	knows how to surf the Internet	has ridden a horse
rides a bus to school	has won a trophy or award	can speak another language	has been to the ocean	has been on a cruise

78

Interview a Friend

Pair each student with a partner, and give each student an Interview a Friend reproducible (page 118). Have students take turns asking each other the questions on the list. Encourage students to record their partner's answers as they go. When everyone has finished their discussion, bring the group together in a circle and talk about what students have in common. Discuss interesting facts they learned about each other.

The Newspaper Stand

Divide the class into teams of three or four. Give each team a small piece of newspaper—a half-sheet works well. Tell each group that they must devise a way to have all the members of their team stand on the paper at the same time while singing "Row, Row, Row Your Boat." No one will be allowed to touch the floor or any other piece of classroom furniture. Allow teams about ten minutes to experiment with different ways of accomplishing this goal. When the practice time is up, have each group share their strategy by putting their team in place and singing.

Build the Eighth Wonder

Divide the class into small groups. Provide each group with an equal number of small marshmallows, a handful of dried spaghetti pasta, and a handful of toothpicks. Tell students they have been selected as architects to design a model of the eighth wonder of the world. This magnificent new creation must take the form of a tower. Their job is to use these "tools" to effectively construct the most creative, well-planned model they can. They must also keep in mind that the taller the tower, the more impressed the judges will be. Teams must work together, and all members must be in agreement over the design and construction of the tower. Groups should begin by making sketches and plans. Present each group with a Certificate of Merit (page 119) for designing and constructing the eighth wonder of the world. Display the projects for other classes and school administrators to view.

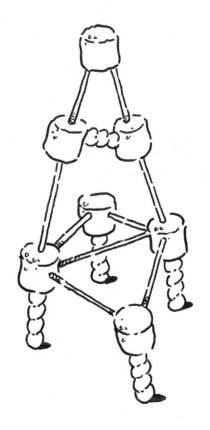

79

School's Cool

Oftentimes, a great deal of knowledge gets "packed away" over summer vacation. Help students shake out the cobwebs and get back in the swing of learning with this fun language-arts activity. Review the definitions of the parts of speech, and make sure students understand each item. Next, give each student a Word List reproducible (page 120). Give students a few minutes to write appropriate kinds of words next to each part of speech on the list, and then give each student a School's Cool reproducible (page 121). Have students copy their words into the correct blanks. Ask students to take turns reading their story for the class. Everyone will enjoy a laugh at these funny stories.

Understand the Pledge of Allegiance

Most students recite the Pledge of Allegiance each day but may not know the meaning of the words they are saying. This activity will help students understand the meaning of the ideas behind the Pledge of Allegiance. Begin by writing the pledge on a piece of chart paper. Ask students to read the words slowly and carefully. Use a red marker to circle all the words that students may not be familiar with. Ask groups of students to use a dictionary to look up the difficult words. Write the definitions on the chart paper using a different-colored marker. Discuss any phrases students may not be familiar with and come to a group understanding of those phrases. Using this piece of chart paper as a guide, work with students to rewrite the Pledge of Allegiance in the class's own words. Neatly copy the student version on a large piece of paper. Display this

class pledge in the room, and have students read it each day before reciting the official Pledge of Allegiance. Students will understand the words they are saying and the meaning behind them.

Investigate School History

Have students investigate the history of their school building. When was the school built? For whom was the school named and why? What were the names of past principals and teachers? Can any of these past staff members be located and interviewed about the school's history? Divide students into research teams. Assign each group one aspect of the school's history to investigate, or let students select their own research topics. Have students create a class presentation about the history of the school based on speeches, videos, slide shows, old pictures in collages, newspaper clippings, and any other media students can find. Have the class present the school history to groups of students, parents, and community members.

Take a Closer Look

Students often overlook the architecture and details of the building where they attend school. Encourage students to see their school through the eyes of an artist. Begin by showing students examples of sketch art. Discuss the intricate details used in sketching, and note how shading is used to achieve effects of shadow and light. Give each student a few sheets of plain paper, a couple of sharpened pencils, and a clipboard. Lead students on a walk around the school, and stop at a spot that is safe and comfortable, like the playground or front lawn. Ask students to spend a few minutes just observing the details of the building, paying attention to architectural details, plants, trees, angles, shadows, and any other important visual information. After students have had sufficient time to observe, ask them to make a sketch. Students may select to draw the entire building or any one architectural detail they find interesting. Some may choose to draw just the door or a piece of decorative sculpture by

the door. Challenge students to be thorough, but not to worry about perfection. They should focus on sketching the building or detail *the way they see it*. When students have completed their sketches, display them in a prominent location, and invite others to a showing of the masterpieces.

81

Create a School Web

Create a word web on chart paper. In the center of the web, write the words *Our School*. Show five lines coming from the center. Label the lines *taste, sight, smell, sound,* and *touch*. Ask students to close their eyes and consider the smells and sounds that remind them of school. Ask them to open their eyes and think about the sights that surround them in school, and then ask them to think about the way things in school feel. Finally, ask them to think about tastes that remind them of school. Ask each student to copy the web onto construction paper. Next, have students list sensory details next to the corresponding lines on their web. Ask students to use the web as a guide to write a sensory paragraph describing their school. Have students share their writing with the rest of the class.

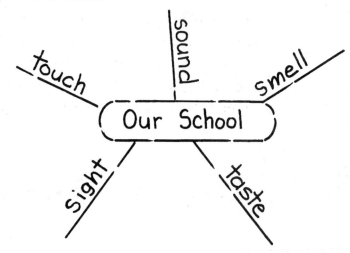

Make Classroom Comparisons

Provide each student with one or two copies of the Open Book reproducible (page 122). Write the following simile introductions on the chalkboard:

Math is like . . .
Social studies is like . . .
Science is like . . .
Writing is like . . .
Reading is like . . .
Spelling is like . . .

Teach a mini-lesson on similes, comparisons of two unlike things, to refresh students' memories. Ask students to choose one or two of the simile starters from the board and think about what that curricular area means to them. Have students finish the comparison by describing their feelings about that particular subject. Invite students to write one comparison on the left side of each reproducible and add an illustration of it on the right side. Display these pages around the room.

Host a Back-to-School Night

Back-to-School Night goes by different names and is scheduled at various times from school district to school district, and sometimes even within a district. The overall objective of the night is to give parents an overview of what their children will be learning and doing that year, give them a chance to get to know you a little, and allow you to reach out to them. The following tips and activities are written as if you will be addressing parents in your own classroom and can be easily adapted for use by a group of teachers addressing an entire grade level.

Prepare for Back-to-School Night

There are so many things you will want to pack into your presentation that organizing it may seem a daunting task. However, if you plan well, you should be able to cover the important points in an interesting and under-standable manner. Inform, but don't over-whelm your audience. Remember that this meeting is designed to give parents an overview of the year, not to discuss every great and inspiring activity you have outlined in your plan book. Make a list of what you want to tell parents. (See page 84 for a sample list.) Prepare handouts ahead of time, and put them in a folder for each parent. These handouts should review everything you will cover in your Back-to-School Night presentation. Include a table of contents at the front, and maintain a professional look to the packet. If you have a favorite handout that is a copy of a copy of a copy (and looks it), retype it and add updated artwork. Keep the masters in a file folder so you can use them again next year.

 Create your own business cards on colored card stock, and laminate them. Include your name, school name, grade level, room number, and the school phone number (or a voice mail or home phone number, if you are comfortable with this). Stick a magnetic strip to the back of each card so parents can keep it on their refrigerator. Attach your business card to your Back-to-School Night parent information packet. It is a personal touch that parents appreciate.

Back-to-School Night Presentation Topics

As time permits, choose from the following topics for your Back-to-School Night presentation:

- curriculum for the first grading period (and the entire year, if you know it)

- field trips and related rules

- daily schedule

- school procedures (e.g., signing in at the office before you visit the classroom)

- brief description of the classroom rules and how you enforce them

- homework

- lunch procedures

- supplies

- labels for anything child brings to school

- book orders

- special events for the year

- dismissal procedure/school rules related to going home

- guidelines for birthday celebrations

- enrichment classes (e.g., computers, foreign languages, music, art)

- how parents can

  - volunteer in the classroom

  - help their child become an independent/self-motivated learner (show How Parents Help reproducibles, pages 123–124)

  - teach responsibility at home

  - read at home

  - build independent/self-motivated students

The Back-to-School Night Parent Packet

Include in your Back-to-School Night parent packet any information that involves parents in their child's education, such as

- How Parents Help reproducibles (pages 123–124)

- copy of the report card

- list of goals related to the report card

- brief outline of your curriculum for the year

- daily schedule

- brief description of the classroom rules and how you enforce them

- information about book orders

- school calendar

- map of the school

- list of upcoming field trips

- student medical release forms

- parent driver insurance forms (or other forms required for parents who volunteer to drive for field trips, if your school does not provide busses for field trips)

- field-trip permission slips (if you already scheduled your trips)

- recommended book list for students

- recommended book list for parents (titles related to parenting students of appropriate age level)

- list of volunteer opportunities for your classroom

- sample of the handwriting style guide your school uses

- school phone numbers

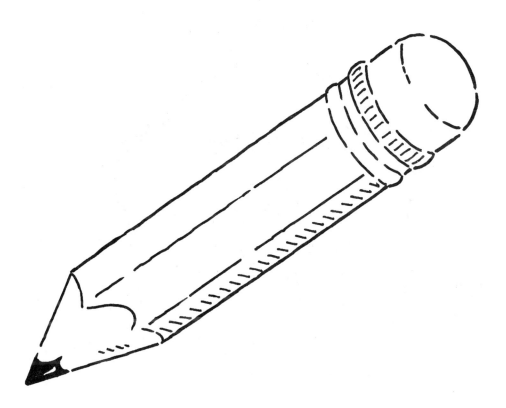

85

Volunteer Job Fair

List all the volunteer positions you anticipate needing to fill during the course of the year. Write a short job description for each position, including specific talents needed for the job, the amount of time required to fill the position, and any special equipment that may be necessary. Type these job descriptions in the form of a classified section of a newspaper. Be creative in your descriptions. Send the classified section home with students just prior to Back-to-School Night. Notify parents that you will be displaying more information about each job at a "Volunteer Job Fair" at Back-to-School Night. Set up a display for each position. Have students help plan and create each display. Include pictures from past years (if available) showing volunteers at work. Include a sign-up sheet at each display, and request that parents make their volunteer choices that evening.

Student Goal Guess

The day of Back-to-School Night, pass out a Student Goal Guess reproducible (page 125) to each student. Read through the list of goals, and ask students to rank them in order of importance in their own lives. (One is most important and five is least important.) Collect the goal sheets, fold each sheet in half, and write the student's name on the outside. Place the goal sheet inside each student's desk. After school, place a new copy of the same reproducible on top of each student's desk. When parents enter the room in the evening, have them sit at their child's desk. Ask parents to read through the goal list and prioritize the goals they have for their child. After they have finished the exercise, have them take out their child's sheet and compare the two lists. Collect the goal sheets, and place them in each student's portfolio.

 Invite parents to sign up as substitute volunteers in case of another parent's absence. With permission, collect the volunteers' phone numbers and distribute them at your training night. Ask parents to call for a sub when they are unable to come to the classroom.

Provide Student-Made Door Prizes

Give each student craft objects (e.g., paper-towel tubes, pipe cleaners, paper, paint, sequins, and glue). Have students create pieces of art to be used as door prizes for Back-to-School Night. Ask them to write a short description of what the art is and copy the description onto an index card. Place the pieces of art and their descriptions on display in the room. Make a copy of the Door Prize Tickets reproducible (page 126). If you need more tickets, make additional copies, use correction fluid to cover the numbers, and write new numbers in sequence. When parents enter the room, tear a ticket in half. Give each parent half of a ticket, and place the other half in a hat or jar for the door-prize drawing later. Draw numbers from the hat each time you start to explain a new section in your presentation, or give away the door prizes at the end of your talk.

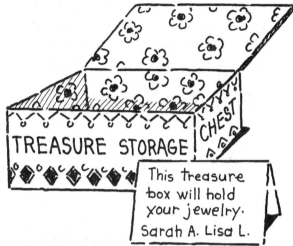

Send Home Student-Made Invitations

Have students create personalized invitations for their parents inviting them to Back-to-School Night. Give students an overview of the agenda you will be using so they can highlight important features of the evening. Encourage students to be creative with their invitation. Some may wish to include illustrations. Others may choose to write a paragraph or poem about why parents should attend. For those students who are musically inclined, invite them to write a singing telegram and deliver it to their parents after school. No matter what form the invitation takes, parents are more likely to attend a function when they have been personally invited by their child.

 Give parents a 3" x 5" (7.5 cm x 12.5 cm) index card as they enter the room for Back-to-School Night. Ask them to write their name, their child's name, and one goal they have for their child this year. Collect the cards, and file them. Use them as discussion starters at parent/teacher conferences.

Host a Back-to-School Night

Ask for Parent Input

Parents are your greatest resource in learning about the students in your class. They have insights and perspectives that you will never uncover in the classroom. Take advantage of their knowledge by asking for their input at Back-to-School Night. Give each child's parent a Parent Input reproducible (page 127). Ask that parents take a few minutes to fill out the survey and return it to you before they leave.

Collect the forms that evening because the likelihood of having them returned greatly diminishes once they leave your room. Ensure parents that their responses will be kept confidential. Invite them to share any additional information they feel would be important for you to know, but is not referred to on the given form. File these forms in a safe location, and refer to them throughout the year.

Make a Parent Message Board

Involve parents in an activity that they will enjoy and their children will love. Cover your door with a large sheet of butcher paper. Attach different-colored markers to the door by tying them with string and knotting the string to the hinges of the door. Invite parents to sign in before or after the presentation. Have them write notes of encouragement to their child or the whole class. Students will love reading the messages from their parents the next morning.

Don't Worry, Be Happy

Keep the following tips in mind for a Back-to-School Night free from worries:

■ Do not worry about making a good first impression. Focus on being enthusiastic, positive, and friendly and you will be a big hit!

■ Do not worry about your classroom being perfect. Post one example of each student's work and you are covered.

■ Do not worry about having the entire year mapped out. Share student goals for the first grading period and keep them simple.

■ Do not worry about giving all of the details of how discipline problems will be handled. Focus on the positive way you approach teaching and how it minimizes problem situations.

■ Do not worry. If you stay focused on sharing with the parents that their children are your top priority and that by working together you can make it a great year for their kids, then everybody will be happy!

Look to the Finish Line

At the end of the year, you will barely remember how young your students seemed when you met them on the first day of school. You will all have come a long way (no matter how many times you may have made the school-year journey before), and you should honor that growth. Students will grow by inches and pounds and be astonished by the math, reading, and writing skills they have gained. Use the following easy-to-implement activities at the beginning of the year, and encourage students to reflect on all their changes at the end of the year.

Start a Slide Show

Consider taking some pictures during the year using slide film. View each developed slide and clearly label it with the date and a key word or phrase describing the picture. Store the slides in a shoe box. Invite parents to take slides during the year and donate them to your class collection. As the year progresses, make a note of any special music or songs that have meaning to your class. Keep this list with the slides. Begin preparing a slide show about a month before school ends. Make tapes of the music you wish to use, and organize your photos in a logical order. Run through the slides with music, and write a script for any narration you wish to include. Share the slide show with parents and students at an end-of-the-year party.

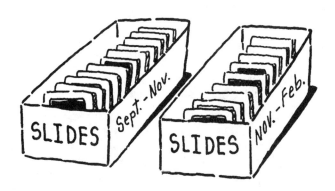

Dear Me

Have students write two letters to themselves, one to be opened at the midpoint in the year and the other to be opened at the end of the year. Encourage students to think about what goals they hope they will have met at each point during the year. Collect the completed letters and store them until the appropriate time in the year. Ask students who enter your room midyear to complete a "Dear Me" letter during their first week at school. Have an opening ceremony where students receive their letters and discuss how they have grown during the year.

Begin a Class Yearbook

If you take lots of photos throughout the year, why not use them to create a class yearbook? Parents appreciate this project and students love to reminisce about the year. To begin this project, develop a file of pictures you take during the school year. Sort your photos as soon as you have the film developed, and label them with a short description of the event in the picture. This will make organizing the yearbook much simpler at the end of the year. Label file folders with the following topics:

- in-class photos

- student project and work photos

- field trips and outings

- assemblies

- miscellaneous

Place labeled photos into the file folder that most closely describes each shot. About a month before school ends, organize a group of students and parents who are willing to help plan the yearbook. Schedule meetings before or after school, or have working lunches. Work together to select the photos you will use in the yearbook. Create volunteer groups to complete different jobs. For example, have one group write a paragraph about each of the photo topics and another group paste the photos and text on plain paper for copying. Assign one group the task of copying and collating the yearbooks and another team designing and producing the cover. Laminate the front and back covers for durability. When the pages are complete, bind them together using a book-binder machine. Your students will be thrilled to have a yearbook of their class documenting all the great things they did during the year.

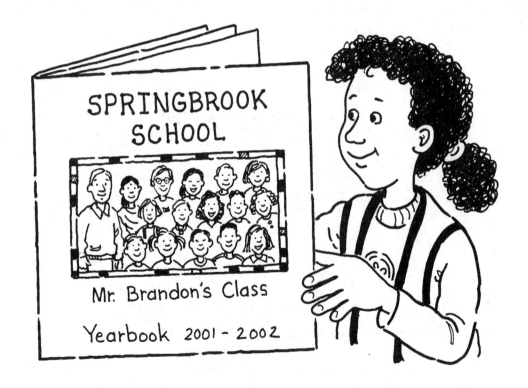

 Use the computer equipment available in your school to assist you with the production of your class yearbook. Use a digital camera to take and store photos throughout the year. Use a scanner to scan photos directly onto the yearbook pages.

Make a Time Capsule

Students like to see how their likes and dislikes change over the course of the year. Help them record this information and seal it away. Provide each student with a 9$\frac{1}{2}$" x 12$\frac{1}{2}$" (24 cm x 31.5 cm) envelope. These envelopes will be their "time capsules." Give each student a Time Capsule reproducible (page 128). Have students fill in each category on the sheet. When you put together the time capsule, ask students to select a few samples of work from each of the curricular areas that they completed during the first weeks of school. During this same time, invite parents to write a note to their child to include in the time capsule. Explain to parents that their child will not read the notes until spring. Have students seal their work, their time capsule form, and the note from their parents in their envelope. Collect the envelopes, and place them in a box. Wrap the box with wrapping paper. Write *Do not open until (date of the end-of-the-year party)* on the box. Put the box on a high shelf until the date you have chosen. On that day, remove the box from the shelf and invite the students to open it as a class. Have students open their time capsule and compare the work they did at the beginning of the year to the work they are doing at the end of the year. Everyone will enjoy noting the students' progress.

Suggested contents for time capsules include
- photograph of the student.

- sample of the student's writing.

- sample of the student's drawing.

- cassette of the student reading.

- picture of his or her family drawn by student.

- end-of-the-year math test. (Have student take the test in September for the time capsule and again at the end of the school year for comparison.)

- index card with the student's height and weight.

 Keep copies of the Time Capsule reproducible handy for students who enter your classroom mid-year. Place these new additions in a manila envelope, and tape the envelope to the top of the time capsule box to be opened at the end of the year.

Trash to Treasure

Dear Parents,

It has been said that, "One person's trash is another person's treasure." We are busy stocking our classroom shelves and preparing for some imaginative learning this year. Please look over the list below. The highlighted items are "trash" that our class would treasure. If you can send any of the items on this list to school with your child we would be very grateful!

age-appropriate games	magazines
aluminum foil	mail-order catalogs
assorted dried pasta	metal cookie/baking trays
baby-food jars	newspaper
baby-wipe boxes	paper bags (any size)
bars of soap	paper plates and cups
blankets	paper-towel rolls
buttons	plastic bags (any size)
carpet samples	plastic bottles
clean milk cartons (any size)	plastic containers with lids (any size)
coffee cans with lids	plastic silverware
craft sticks	rice
dried beans	sheets
drinking straws	shoe boxes (any size)
egg cartons	stationery or postcards
empty cans (soup or juice)	stencils
envelopes	toothpicks
fabric scraps	twist ties
felt	used greeting cards
fiberfill	wallpaper samples
food coloring	wood scraps
game pieces (e.g., dice, tokens, chips)	yarn

Please do not send anything you would like returned. We plan to use it ALL!

Thank you,

Back to School • 4–6 • © 2000 Creative Teaching Press

Year-at-a-Glance

Subject _____   School Year _____

August	September	October	November	December	January
February	March	April	May	June	July

Volunteer Guidelines

Thank you so much for volunteering in the classroom. You are a valued part of our school family. I know your time in our classroom will be very rewarding for you, and it will be a tremendous help to us.

Please keep a few things in mind when you are working with the students.

- Please check in with the front office.

- Be positive with the students and with the work that they do. Maintain realistic standards for their work.

- Feel free to help a student. However, we encourage students to do all the work. Students learn by experimenting . . . so let them do their work if at all possible. Ask them first, "What do you think you should do?"

- Remember to keep what happens in the classroom in the room. Please don't discuss the lives or learning of the students you assist with other students or adults who are not in the classroom. On the other hand, if you have a concern, please feel free to bring it to my attention immediately.

- Please remember to be on time. If you are unable to come at your scheduled time, please call the office, send a note, or try calling someone else on the volunteer list to see if he or she can substitute for you. We do depend on you.

- Try to stay as professional as possible. Please keep in mind that we are always role models for the students.

- Have fun with the students and enjoy yourself!

Lists

Survival List

- [ ] _____
- [ ] _____
- [ ] _____
- [ ] _____
- [ ] _____
- [ ] _____
- [ ] _____
- [ ] _____
- [ ] _____
- [ ] _____
- [ ] _____
- [ ] _____
- [ ] _____
- [ ] _____
- [ ] _____
- [ ] _____
- [ ] _____
- [ ] _____
- [ ] _____

Book Order Parent Letter

Dear Parents,

Attached is the book order for the month of _____. Here are three great books you might consider for your child's collection this month.

1.

2.

3.

Please send exact change or a check made payable to _____, along with the completed order form in an envelope. Print your child's name and room number on the order form. Turn in all orders no later than _____ if you wish to order books this month.

Thank you,

Check when done:
☐ I have marked the books I wish to order.
☐ Child's name is on the order form.
☐ Exact change or a check is in the envelope.

Reminder Chart

Reminder—
Things to Consider
When Solving Your Problem

Read through these points, and answer each question in your mind.

1. Take a minute to get yourself under control. Take three deep breaths.

2. Think about what happened.

3. What events led up to the conflict?

4. What actions did you take that caused the conflict?

5. What actions did you take to prevent the conflict?

6. What can you do to solve the problem?

7. What can you do to prevent this from happening again?

Invitation

Dear Parents and Students,

You are cordially invited to a Room-Warming Party! The first day of school is just around the corner. What better way to get the year started right than to pitch in and get to know each other while we create a great learning space for the year?

Refreshments will be provided!

I have set aside two days next week for the room setup. In order to make our time together more productive, I have divided the class alphabetically into groups. This way we will have plenty of room to work and plenty of jobs to keep everyone busy. I understand if you are unable to attend due to a scheduling conflict. You will be missed.

Day 1:

Last Name	Time
A–F	
G–L	

Day 2:

Last Name	Time
M–S	
T–Z	

I look forward to meeting you and having you help get our room in shape.

Sincerely,

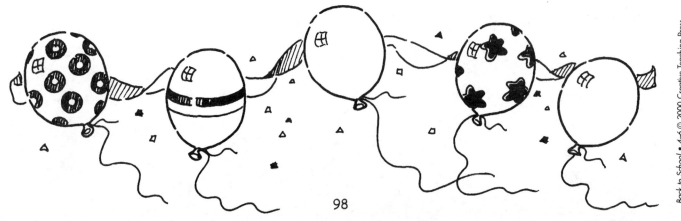

Back to School • 4–6 © 2000 Creative Teaching Press

Something about Me

Dear _____,

I am looking forward to working with you this year. We have a great many things to learn and discover together. I would like to take this opportunity to learn a few things about you before the first day of school. Please take a few minutes to answer the following questions and return them to me in the self-addressed, stamped envelope in this packet.

1. Tell me your favorite school memory.

2. List three things you do well.

3. What is the most exciting thing you've ever done?

4. How do you feel about school? Why?

5. What is one wish you have for this school year?

6. What is one thing you want me to know about you?

Sincerely,

Signature Log

Date	Comments	Parent Signature

Contact

Student_____ Birthdate _____

Mailing Address _____

Parents/Guardians _____

Best Times to Call _____

Home Phone _____ Work Phone _____

Emergency Contact _____ Phone _____

Special Information_____

Date _____ Whom Contacted _____

How: Phone   Note w/ Child   Mail   In Person

Summary _____

_____

_____

_____

Date _____ Whom Contacted _____

How: Phone   Note w/ Child   Mail   In Person

Summary _____

_____

_____

_____

Date _____ Whom Contacted _____

How: Phone   Note w/ Child   Mail   In Person

Summary _____

_____

_____

_____

Classroom Scavenger Hunt

1. Write the title and author of four books found in the classroom library.

2. What brand of soap is found at the sink?

3. What is the capital city of Montana?

4. How many chairs are in the classroom?

5. What are the length and height of each chalkboard found in the room?

6. What does the word *mosasaur* mean?

7. How many steps does it take to get from your desk to the classroom door?

8. Name three software programs on the classroom computer.

9. Find out if your classroom has a film or slide projector. If so, where is it?

10. How many encyclopedias are in the classroom?

Schultute

School children in Germany are given a large paper cone filled with candy and school supplies on their first day of school. The goody-filled cone is called a *Schultute* (pronounced *shool-'tootuh*). It symbolizes the wish that the students will have a rich education in the years ahead. Use the following directions to make your own *Schultute*.

Step 1: Cut the cone shape out of the paper provided by your teacher.

Step 2: Decorate the cone using crayons or markers. Draw scenes and symbols that are related to school.

Step 3: When you have finished decorating, roll the paper into a cone. Have a partner help you staple the cone closed.

Step 4: Punch two holes in the top of the cone. Use yarn to make a handle for your cone.

Step 5: Place the decorated cone on your desk before you leave for lunch.

Cone Shape

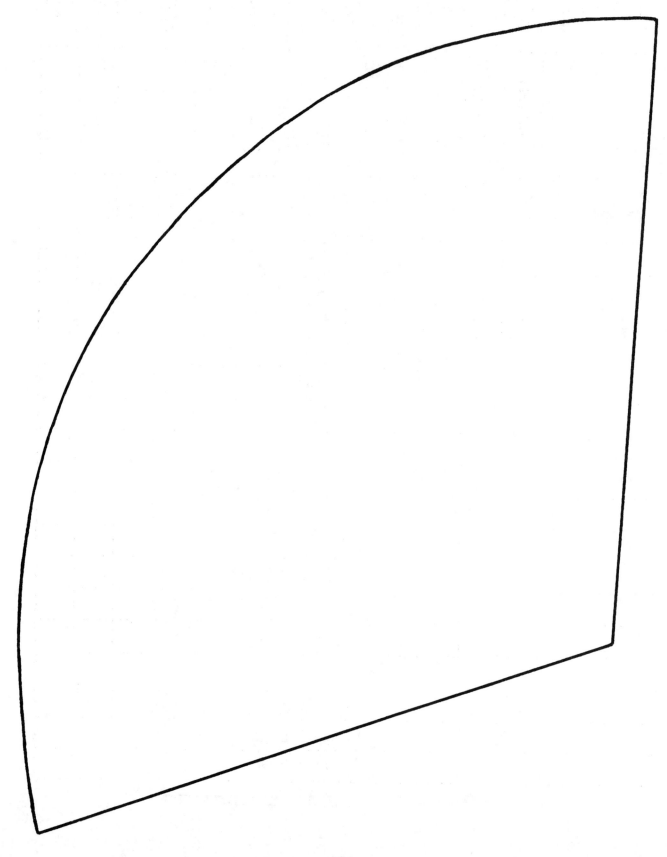

School Supply Checklist

Name	Supplies	crayons	glue	tissue	pencils	ruler	eraser	markers				

Times of Our Lives

_____

_____

_____

_____

_____

_____

_____

_____

_____

_____

_____

Goals for Success

We Missed You

Name_____ Date _____

While you were out, you missed some important work. Please make up the work and turn it in by the date written on the bottom of this sheet. If you have questions or need help, please see me.

Subject	Assignment	✓ When Completed

Due date_____

Name _____   Date _____

Assignment Account

Date	Assignment

Missing Assignment Form

Student Name_____ Date _____

Missing Assignment _____

_____

_____

Parent Signature_____ Student Signature _____

- -

Missing Assignment Form

Student Name_____ Date _____

Missing Assignment _____

_____

_____

Parent Signature_____ Student Signature _____

Get Your Child on Track

Here are a few suggestions your child can use at home to organize school materials and complete assignments on time. Read through the ideas with your child and display the list in a prominent place. Spend some time with your child establishing good study habits and the school year will be a great success.

1. Establish one central location at home for doing homework.

2. Place your backpack and materials at your "study station" when you arrive home from school.

3. Establish a specific study time each night, such as when you arrive home, after dinner, or early evening.

4. Review your assignment notebook at the beginning of your study time.

5. Mark an X in front of each assignment as you complete it.

6. Check through your completed assignments and your notebook with a parent.

7. Carefully repack your backpack with your completed assignments and your materials.

8. Place your backpack by the door through which you will leave for school in the morning.

Rate Your Group

Assignment or Project Name_____

1. Write two things you learned while working in this group.

2. How well did you perform in your group?

        1   2   3   4   5

    Great   Not Well

3. How well did your group work together?

        1   2   3   4   5

    Great   Not Well

4. If you were to work with this group again, what would you do differently to improve your group's performance?

Student Signature_____

Back to School • 4-6 © 2000 Creative Teaching Press

Name_____ Date _____

Alternate Solution Sheet

What is the problem? Describe it. (Who was involved? Where did it happen?
What do you remember happened?)

What steps did you take to solve the problem?

Was the problem solved?   YES   NO

What would you like to have happen now?

Student Signature_____ Teacher Signature_____

Cool Coupons

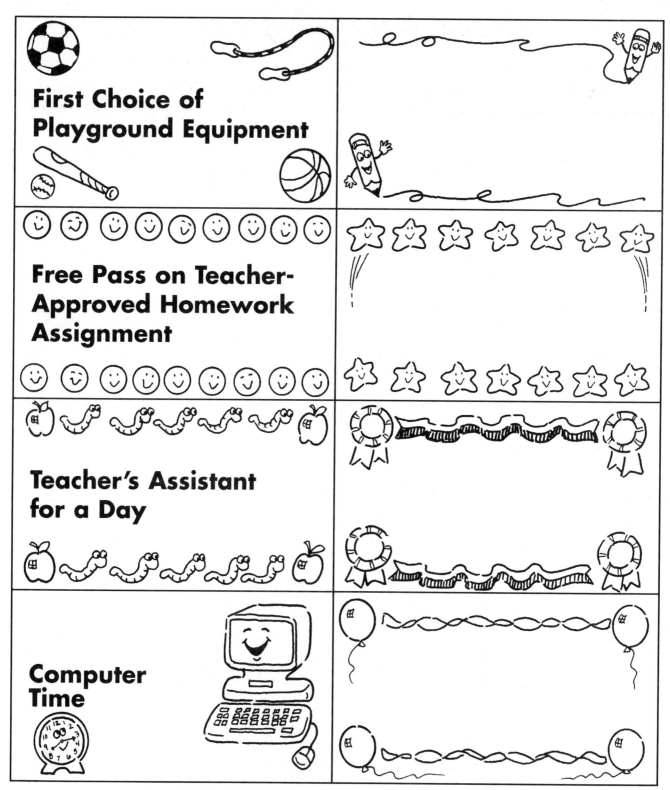

First Choice of Playground Equipment

Free Pass on Teacher-Approved Homework Assignment

Teacher's Assistant for a Day

Computer Time

Back to School • 4–6 © 2000 Creative Teaching Press

Name _____ Week beginning _____

How Am I Doing?

Task	Mon.	Tue.	Wed.	Thurs.	Fri.

Kid Watch

Name _____

Week beginning _____

Language Arts

Math

Other

Comments

Parent Signature _____

Teacher Signature _____

116

Name_____ Date _____

Find Someone Who . . .

Directions: Get a signature in each box. Each person may sign no more than twice.

plays a musical instrument	has a pet	plays a sport	belongs to a club or group	has lived in another state
_____	_____	_____	_____	_____
has lived in another country	has a special collection	has been in a contest	has grown something in a garden	has an unusual hobby
_____	_____	_____	_____	_____
has two or more brothers	has two or more sisters	likes to keep their room clean	wants to become a professional athlete	has been stung by a bee
_____	_____	_____	_____	_____
loves math	took a summer school class	read at least two books over the summer	knows how to surf the Internet	has ridden a horse
_____	_____	_____	_____	_____
rides a bus to school	has won a trophy or an award	can speak another language	has been to the ocean	has been on a cruise
_____	_____	_____	_____	_____

Back to School • 4–6 © 2000 Creative Teaching Press

Name_____ Date _____

Interview a Friend

1. If everything in your bedroom had to be one color, what color would you make it? Why?	
2. If you could take only one book on a very long journey, what book would it be? Why?	
3. If you could have any talent in the world, what would you choose? Why?	
4. If you could buy anything in the world, what would you buy? Why?	
5. If you could be a famous artist, what would you create? Why?	
6. If you could have any pet, what would you choose? Why?	
7. If you could change one thing about yourself, what would it be? Why?	
8. If you could be granted one wish, what would it be? Why?	
9. If you could compete in the Olympics, what event would you choose? Why?	
10. If you were being sent to outer space and could only take three items, what would you choose? Why?	

Certificate of Merit

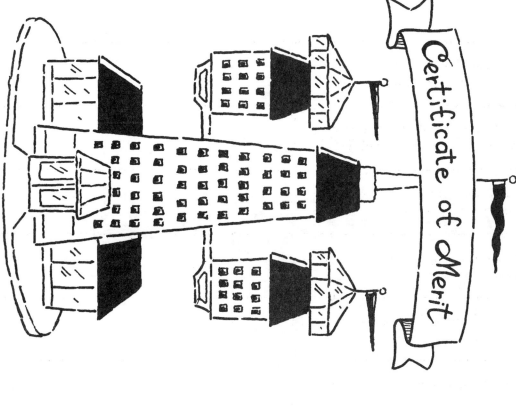

Design Team
for the
Eighth Wonder of the World

Team Name _____

Team Members _____

_____

_____

_____

Judge's Signature _____

Back to School • 4–6 © 2000 Creative Teaching Press

Word List

1. adjective _____

2. verb _____

3. adjective _____

4. proper noun _____

5. noun _____

6. plural noun _____

7. plural noun _____

8. past-tense verb _____

9. number _____

10. proper noun _____

11. noun _____

12. plural noun _____

13. famous person _____

Back to School • 4–6 © 2000 Creative Teaching Press

School's Cool

Today was my first day at _____ School. What a place!
(1)

When the bell rang, everyone started to _____. My teacher's
(2)

name was Mr./Mrs._____. I had to sit next to _____,
(3)   (4)

the class _____!
(5)

"No yelling, no running, and no chewing _____," the teacher
(6)

said. "And remember, every student must have notebooks, pencils, and

_____."
(7)

I nearly _____ when the teacher said, "Read _____ books
(8)   (9)

by tomorrow, including *The Wizard of* _____ and *Charlotte's*
(10)

_____."
(11)

At last the final bell rang. The school bus pulled up filled with

_____, and guess who was driving—_____!
(12)   (13)

Open Book

How Parents Help

Many things that you do at home on a daily basis will help your children the most. The activties described below benefit all children.

1. Set aside a special reading time. Tell your child you look forward to and enjoy your reading time together. Try reading chapter books with an older children.

2. Let your child see you reading. Read the newspaper, magazines, and books in front of your child.

3. Listen to your child. Oral language experiences strengthen children's reading.

4. Talk with your child.

5. Make time to play with and enjoy your child—regardless of his or her age.

6. Begin to solve problems *with* your child, not *for* him or her.

7. Invite your child to complete household chores and projects with you. Discuss how and why you do certain things, and explain all the details to your child.

8. Encourage your child to write letters to relatives and friends.

9. Praise your child whenever possible.

10. Supervise homework. Give your child a place to work, and check that assignments are completed.

11. Talk with your child about school and everyday events.

12. Encourage exercise and good nutrition.

13. Broaden your child's horizons by taking him or her to parks, museums, libraries, zoos, historical sites, and sporting events.

14. Tell your child education is important, and encourage him or her to do well in school.

15. Children will know intuitively how to behave; teach your child kindly, but firmly.

16. Help your child get a library card from the public library. Take your child to the library as often as possible.

17. Help your child pick out interesting books to read.

18. Talk to your child about subjects that are interesting to him or her.

19. Write notes to your child. Leave them to be found in special places—under pillows, in lunches, or in favorite books.

How Parents Help

Page 2

20. Give your child a place to keep his or her own books.

21. Encourage your child to keep a scrapbook about a subject that interests him or her (e.g., stamps, dogs, birds, trucks, photos of the family doing activities together).

22. Limit your child's television watching. Turn on the television for a specific show and turn it off immediately after the show is over.

23. Read and discuss your child's schoolwork together.

24. Provide materials for creative projects (e.g., crayons, pencils, paper, paint, scissors).

25. Help your child write down special events on a calendar and mark off each day.

26. Help your child make a telephone directory with the names and telephone numbers of friends and relatives.

27. Encourage your child to play outside and get plenty of fresh air.

28. Invite your child to help you prepare dinner or bake a special treat.

29. Subscribe to a children's magazine in your child's name.

30. Bring books in the car for your child to read.

31. Look up words in the dictionary with your child.

32. Encourage your child to show his or her schoolwork to your friends and relatives.

33. When traveling, read road signs with your child and discuss what they mean. Play road-sign games.

34. Show your child how to use a yardstick, ruler, or tape measure to measure things around the house.

35. Give your child a special place to keep items he or she must take to school regularly.

36. Display your child's work around your house.

37. Hug your child daily!

Back to School • 4–6 © 2000 Creative Teaching Press

Student Goal Guess

Rank each goal in order of importance.

1—most important   5—least important

_____I will work to keep my desk and locker in order.

_____I will work to turn in my assignments on time.

_____I will work to improve my athletic abilities.

_____I will work to improve my math skills.

_____I will try to make new friends.

Door Prize Tickets

Parent Input

Dear Parents,

Please assist me in getting to know your child by completing the following survey. Providing information and reflections about your child will help me better meet his or her educational needs. It will also enable me to work with you to create the best learning environment for your child both at school and at home. Your responses will remain confidential.

Child's Name:

Parents' or Guardians' Names:

List three of your child's strengths:

1.

2.

3.

What is one area in which your child needs improvement? _____

My child is interested in _____.

As a family, we like to _____.

Academically this year, I would like to see my child _____.

Socially this year, I would like to see my _____.

Something I would like to share with you about my child is _____

_____

_____.

Please use the back of this paper to provide any other information that you feel is important for me to know.

Thank you,

Time Capsule

Name_____

Birthdate_____ Height_____ Weight_____ Shoe Size_____

Hobbies_____

Favorites:

    Food _____

    Song _____

    TV Show _____

    Movie _____

    Book _____

    Sport _____

    Friends _____

    Celebrities _____

What I like to do on weekends: _____

Four things I like most:

    1.

    2.

    3.

    4.

Four things I like least:

    1.

    2.

    3.

    4.

Favorite subject in school: _____

By the end of the year, I want to_____.

Back to School • 4–6 © 2000 Creative Teaching Press